slumgirl dreaming

RUBINA'S JOURNEY TO THE STARS

RUBINA ALI

in collaboration with Anne Berthod and Divya Dugar

DELACORTE PRESS

All rights reserved. Published in the United States by
Delacorte Press, an imprint of Random House Children's Books,
a division of Random House, Inc., New York.
Originally published in French by Oh! Editions, Paris, in 2009.
First English publication in paperback by
Transworld Publishers, Ltd., London, in 2009.

Delacorte Press is a registered trademark and the colophon
is a trademark of Random House, Inc.

Visit us on the Web! www.randomhouse.com/teens

Educators and librarians, for a variety of teaching tools, visit us at
www.randomhouse.com/teachers

Library of Congress Cataloging-in-Publication Data
Ali, Rubina.
Slumgirl dreaming : Rubina's journey to the stars / Rubina Ali in collaboration
with Anne Berthod and Divya Dugar.
p.   cm.
ISBN 978-0-385-73908-5 (hardcover) — ISBN 978-0-375-89712-2
(e-book) 1. Ali, Rubina. 2. Motion picture actors and actresses—India—
Biography. 3. Slumdog millionaire (Motion picture). I. Berthod, Anne.
II. Dugar, Divya. III. Title.
PN2888.A42A3 2009
791.430'28092—dc22
[B]
2009029305

The text of this book is set in 12-point Giovanni.

Printed in the United States of America

10 9 8 7 6 5 4 3 2 1

First American Edition

slumgirl dreaming

Ru-bi-na! A-zhar! A-yush! Ta-nay!

I don't understand what's happening. I can hear yelling in the distance, but after twenty hours in the plane I'm really drowsy, and with all the noise and chaos at Mumbai airport I feel completely out of it. The chanting becomes clearer and clearer until there is no doubt left in my mind that people are calling out our names. Around me, my friends Azhar, Ayush and Tanay, the other child actors of *Slumdog Millionaire*, are looking at each other and also wondering what's going on.

We are all walking along the newly mopped floor in Mumbai airport. I walk next to Azhar. We both have brand new shoes that look nice on the clean ground. We've just picked up our suitcases.

We've come off the plane from Los Angeles after *Slumdog Millionaire* picked up eight Oscars. Thursday 26 February is my return from my first ever international trip, to America. I'm so excited about seeing my family. I've never been away from them for so long. I hoped we'd be greeted like celebrities, and it really is happening. Azhar, who played young Salim, looks at me sideways. He has a wild spark in his eyes. I can tell he's as excited as I am. And Ayush, who played Jamal, is jumping up and down with joy. Suddenly, I don't feel tired any more. I want to talk to everyone who wants to talk to me. Azhar's mother glances over at her son; she looks a bit worried. Maybe she wants to protect him. My uncle is tense. He waits for instructions from someone in our group – the production crew or a security guard. He doesn't really know what to do. The last of our bags has been picked up from the conveyor belt, we are through Customs and we are dying to get out.

'Ru-bi-na! A-zhar!'

'A-yush! Ta-nay!'

Outside, people are screaming. Azhar and I can barely keep quiet. I want to shout back, 'Yes, it's me, Rubina!' But we are a bit lost and feeling out of sorts with all the security men bustling round us and shouting. The production crew seem to be discussing something complicated with the airport security. They are pointing at us and at our bags on the trolleys. Police officers come up to us.

'Don't go outside – it's madness out there, and you'll never get through.'

'So what are we supposed to do?'

'Just wait a bit. We're going to clear a passage and make a barricade for you all to get through the crowd.'

Even the police are shocked to see such a crowd. They rub their moustaches and scratch at their uniforms. It is going to be a big project for them to get us all out safely.

'Rubina, I've never seen even the biggest stars or politicians greeted by this many people,' they tell me.

How many people can there be out there? My father and my family must be somewhere among them. My father couldn't accompany me to America, but I know he's outside waiting for me and will take me home. Now I'm anxious to see everyone again: my grandmother, my big sister and my little brother. But I missed my father the most.

At last, a policeman walks over to someone in the crew. He tells us we can go. A dozen policemen go ahead of us, machine guns slung across their chests. Ayush and I follow them, with my uncle holding my hand tight; Azhar's mother is close behind. She is trying to keep up with Azhar, who's in front of her now. Through a window, I see an ocean of people pressing and pushing outside. I have to pinch myself to believe that they all are here for me and the crew. There are hundreds of faces. They are pushing each other and stepping on each other just to try and get a glimpse. I can even see people climbing up a barrier or something so they don't miss any of the show. And the show is us. The security guards are struggling to manage all these people. There are a lot of journalists, too, armed with cameras, mics and lenses as long as your arm.

'Azhaaar! Rubiiiina!'

As we come out of the airport, the cameras click madly and there's a huge push with people calling out from all sides just to get me to say something. What shall I say? There is so much I could tell them. I have seen so much. Ayush and I squeeze against Tanay, not knowing where to look, who to smile at or what to say. But Tanay is concentrating on finding his grandmother, who's holding up an enormous sign above the crowd on which is written in large letters: **WELCOME TANAY**.

'Over here! A little smile, please!'

'How was America, Rubina? Who did you meet?'

'Rubina, listen just a second, please!'

The people are cheering us like we're heroes. The

10

Oscars seem very far away now. I must be living a dream. My dream of being a Bollywood actress, which I have wanted to be all my life. Here I am, barely nine and this dream has come true. With one hand, I hold on to the fluffy little bear I brought back from Los Angeles; with the other, I wave to people as if I was Shahrukh Khan.

Azhar is acting like a monkey, laughing and yelling 'hurrah!' and relishing our first taste of stardom. Thanks to the ropes that are stretched along the pavement, we manage to make our way to the cars, but security is finding it more and more difficult to control the crowd. People are trying to slip between them. I look frantically for my father. I stand on tiptoes trying to see the familiar face of my aba in this mass of people. But I can't make him out.

Some people drape garlands of flowers round our necks and then journalists jam their mics under my chin from all directions. I don't mind it at all – quite the opposite: I feel like a star. Just as we reach these amazing-looking black Mercedes cars, hired by the production team to escort us back to our homes, the crowd manages to break the cordon and suddenly it's a mad rush. There's yelling everywhere, but I can't make out what they are saying any more. The only thing I can hear is: 'Rubina, please! One minute only!'

Azhar has been lifted into the air and suddenly he disappears from view. Then my aba comes towards me, shouting, 'Rubina, *meri jaan*, my love!' and I find myself pressed against my father's chest. As soon as he'd seen me, he'd frantically jostled his way to the front and crawled below the cordon to reach me. He tried to explain to the police that he was my father, but they didn't believe him. 'Yes, today everyone would like to be Rubina's father!' they said to him.

But he managed to get through anyway. Snuggled in his arms, more than a metre above the ground, I look out over this jubilant crowd with delight. My celebrity status seems much nicer when I'm safe in my father's arms. Carried by Aba, I reach the air-conditioned car with my uncle still beside me. Someone opens the door and we sink into the back seat. The windows are rolled up and I can still hear the lingering sound of my name being called out. I smile and giggle that all this is for me and wonder if I really have become such a big star.

Inside the car a surprise is waiting for me: Munni, my stepmother, Dilshad, my aunt, and my grandmother and sister are all squeezed in there. I jump on their laps and kiss them. The pride I can see in their eyes makes me so happy. Munni looks at my new pink dress and fondles the soft material. This is an outfit I bought in Los Angeles. Even my cardigan matches the dark blue of my tights and with this new dress I think I look quite the little American. I chatter away, trying to tell them all about my trip.

I see Azhar get in to another Mercedes with his mother. As the cars start to move, there are still hands and faces pressed up against the dark windows. The journalists run behind us until we reach the main road. My head is buzzing. I sit back on my stepmother's lap, trying to relax in the calm and coolness. But my peace and quiet is not going to last, as my father warns me: 'Aree, you'll see – everyone's waiting for you at home. There are journalists everywhere!'

For a short while, we have a police escort. As soon as we arrive in Bandra, my slum, they'll leave, and I'll go back to my previous life. It's very strange coming back to my little shanty: just a few days ago, I was racing round with Azhar in a hotel room ten times the size of my home. I didn't even know rooms that large existed! But I know my life is not the same any more.

After all the things I've seen and all the luxury and the pampering, I feel confused about going back to the filthy streets of the slums. At the same time, I'm impatient to be with my friends again and see the looks on their faces when I tell them about all the stars I met on the red carpet! I imagine that Azhar must be in the same state of mind – he and I live in the same area and his slum is just across the road. Our lives are pretty similar to those of the characters we played in the film: we've gone from the slums to the stars.

i

Slumgirl

My name is Rubina Ali. I don't know when my birthday is, and nor does my father, but I know I'm nine years old. I was born in Baba Hospital, in Bandra. I've always lived in Bandra East slum. My neighbourhood is called Garib Nagar, 'the area of the poor'. It's not big, but it's still a small city on its own. I am familiar with every nook and cranny of this area. It doesn't look that vast but we have ten thousand inhabitants per square kilometre. Building a shanty town is like doing a jigsaw puzzle out of odds and ends of sheet metal, wooden planks and plastic blue sheets. We make use of every inch of space available to us. Our little huts don't belong to my aba or uncle – it's government land – but people have been living here for many years. This

15

is my world: a bit rough and hardly a movie-star lifestyle.

The slum has a main road running along the railway track, which is the hub of activity. It is always teeming with people. There are children playing, picking up the dirt and rubbish from the railway track, and old and young huddling together to chat and gossip. All the community functions and celebrations take place here. This road also has a barber shop, tea stalls, grocery shops and a video game booth. Many vendors sit next to the railway tracks selling fruit, vegetables and various snacks, such as meat which is full of flies but delicious once cooked. There are also those who set up right on the ground, putting their eggs or spices on a blanket. There's always something going on here. I spend a lot of time playing here and hanging out with my friends. To the north of this road is a wasteland where they empty the rubbish, and to the east is the station where all the trains from the Mumbai suburbs arrive.

We meet, me and my friends and other children, to play games like tag among the goats and chickens and all the people who lounge about in the sun. It's quite rare but sometimes a goods train still goes past, and then there is a frenzy to move the stalls and drying clothes and everyone has to get off the tracks in a hurry, especially the old people who sleep on the ground. I've already seen accidents happen.

The back of the slums is the worst part. It's full of dirty water, poo and muck. No one can walk in that so we've made a path with bricks and wooden planks so people can get through. Beyond that there's a mud mound a few metres high that's all covered in rubbish and poo as well.

As soon as you leave the main street and go in to the narrow alleyways between the metal-roofed houses, everything is dark and humid. The gutter is full of black water and always bubbling with insects. It takes up half the passage. The rest is unsteady paving stones and animal poo, so you have to be careful where you put your feet. But I'm used to it. I've seen many kids fall in these gutters, which I find very funny. Most people leave their door open: then you can see seven or eight people in a single room without a window. That's where you eat, sleep and bathe. There's no privacy in slums. Everyone lives with everyone else, and also with rats, cockroaches and mosquitoes – they are everywhere.

When I was very young, I thought that Mumbai was nothing but slums, wastelands, sewers, stinking water and rickety houses. And then, from watching soap operas and movies on our old black-and-white telly, I became aware of a world outside the slums. The wobbly image on our old television set was my first view of this dream world. Until I went to Hollywood, I'd only left my Bandra slum twice; once for a pilgrimage to the tomb of Ajmer Sharif in Rajasthan when I was three, and once to Kolkata with my stepmother not long ago. I don't remember much about the Rajasthan trip and my trip to Kolkata wasn't that great. The slums where my stepmother Munni comes from are even worse than ours.

My neighbourhood is a mix of interesting people. There is a man who lives opposite our house, who seems quite nice to me. But all the boys make fun of him, calling him *ladki, ladki* (girl, girl). He walks a bit like a girl and doesn't really hang out with the boys on the street. He was about to get married and everything was arranged but then he decided to become a *hijra* (transsexual). Now he wears a sari and begs. If someone laughs at him then he goes mad and shouts insults at them.

Rafiq Qureshi Ali, who I call Aba, is my father, a tall man with a black moustache and curly hair that he dyes with henna to hide the white hairs and to keep his head cool in the summer. Yes, henna has cooling properties! My father is a nice man, who doesn't drink and smoke, like most of the others in the slums do. Lots of people have told me I resemble my father a lot. Whenever I look at myself in the mirror, I feel that my eyes are just like his – big, round and expressive. He is everything to me: father and mother. He was born in Mumbai, too, thirty-six years ago, but in Dharavi slums. They are the biggest slums in Mumbai, much bigger than ours. He spent the first few years of his life there. He says life in Dharavi was very hard, that the children were bullied because of their caste. After that, he went with his parents and two older brothers to live in Kerala, in southern India, where his family originally came from. My grandfather earned his living working as an agent for people who wanted passports. His job was to speed up the process, and to arrange all the documents if the person didn't have them. I never knew him. He died thirty years ago. My grandmother remarried quite soon afterwards, and they eventually came back to Mumbai, to the Bandra East slums.

They lived inside four walls of sheet metal, with no running water or electricity. I think they were even poorer than us. My father did not always have enough to eat. Like me, he was also sent to an Urdu-language school in Dharavi. One day, he told me his secret – that he hated studying and that he always use to skip classes or run away from school to hang around with his friends. The alphabets and numbers didn't make that much sense to him, so he was always lost in his own world even if he attended the class.

He started working very young to help his step-father support the family. Mohiuddin, my father's elder brother, was the first to earn money. He came up with the idea of starting a slum theatre, so he hired a film projector and started organizing movie shows with an admission charge for the neighbours. Gulam, the middle brother, and Rafiq, my father, pulled carts from the age of twelve, transporting bricks or sand to earn a few rupees. Then my father started to work as an apprentice to Akhtar Pathan, a carpenter, who is a slum builder and also repairs chairs and tables. He feels quite indebted to this carpenter, who taught him everything about the trade.

When I was quite young my father told me about his first marriage, to my biological mother Khursheed. He was eighteen. She was a year younger and lived in the same neighbourhood. She was also a devout Muslim. The match was arranged by my father's step-father. They organized a big feast at the main road of our slum and many of my relatives came from far away. The festivities went on for a couple of days. Of course, it wasn't like weddings in films: they just pitched a tent on an empty lot, but it was still a gala affair by slum standards.

Ten months later, they had their first little girl,

but the baby died the next day. My father was very depressed. Sana, my big sister, was born three years later, at Baba Hospital. I was born four years after that. It was Aba who chose my first name at the ceremony. It always happens like that: forty days after a birth, all the close friends and family get together, and everyone proposes a name. Then it's up to the head of the family to make the final decision. Aba didn't even listen to the various suggestions. From the beginning, he knew deep down in his heart that I would be called Rubina. I was a year old when my brother, Abbas, came into the world. I don't remember since I was only a baby. The next year our mother left us and went away with some other man. According to my father, this was no great loss: it seems she didn't really take care of us and was always threatening to leave him for someone else. They fought a lot so finally one day he told her, 'Fine, leave!' Now she has remarried someone not from our caste and lives in the slums of Panvel.

He told me she'd wanted to see us again but he had forbidden it because she wasn't a good mother, otherwise she wouldn't have abandoned us like this. That's why I have no memory of her as my mother. I also know she came back several times to see us, but each time my father drove her away.

'You never took care of your children, so you don't deserve to see them. Go away!'

But I still saw her in the neighbourhood, speaking to other men and laughing with them. I know for sure that she doesn't have a good character.

After the separation, my mother sold the house for about 70,000 rupees and we moved in with Dadi, my paternal grandmother. She lives above the ground floor and the room was a bit bigger than our previous room. The advantage of being higher up is that you don't risk being flooded. During monsoon season, that happens all the time. The gutter overflows, and black water runs into the ground-floor dwellings and the smell is awful. It's really disgusting, even when you're used to it. Three years ago at my uncle and aunt's house the water got a metre and a half high. There were floods in Mumbai and it rained day and night. Everyone stayed in their dwellings as long as they could, hoping the rain would stop. All my aunt and uncle's belongings got damaged, including the bed, mattresses and also the fridge. It was so dirty, because all sorts of disgusting stuff had been floating in the water, that they had to throw all their things away. Then, when the water receded, the walls were left covered in filthy streaks, which had to be scrubbed and scrubbed.

My grandmother's house, like all the others, was

made out of every material possible. In the main room, we hung an old cloth to mark off the area where we washed and did the dishes, on the floor, in the same basin. Dadi did the cooking on a piece of wood balanced on top of a few boxes. Glasses and tin plates were piled on shelves on the wall, and we put our clothes away in a large wardrobe. To sleep, cloth mats were spread out on the floor, and we all huddled up against each other. There were six of us sleeping in that little room. Me, Sana, Abbas, Aba, Dadi and Uncle Gulam, who had been married but his wife and children left him because of his vice of drinking, and now he stayed with us. Mohiuddin, my other uncle, lived a few streets away with his wife, Dilshad, their daughter Rukhsar, who was eleven at the time, and my cousin Mohsin, who was seven.

Since my mother was no longer there, my father took care of us, but with his work, he didn't have much time, so it was Dadi, with Sana's help, who gave me and my brother baths, changed our nappies and prepared our bottles. My brother and I were still too small to fend for ourselves. Dadi got up at dawn every day to get the water. She was lucky to have a tap, just downstairs, which she shared with her neighbours. In the slums, getting water is very hard. The water only runs from five until ten in the morning. You have to get up quite early to queue and fill enough containers to last until the next day. Then she prepared breakfast of *maska pav* (buttered bun), which is one of my favourites, or scrambled eggs with tomatoes and little peppers. At seven, we got up, brushed our teeth and drank our *chai* all together; then my father left for work around nine. He went to the main square with his tools and waited for customers to approach him. As for Uncle Gulam, he ran a tea stall a few streets away.

One day, when I was four and Sana almost eight, my father decided to send us to school. Not many of my friends went to school but Aba was anxious for us to learn to read and write Urdu. Aba told me that this language was started by Muslim rulers in Delhi a very long time ago and that Urdu is one of the official languages in India. The Koran is translated into Urdu, so that's why people want to learn it. My aba told me there are many words common between Urdu and Hindi, which makes it easier to learn as well. So he enrolled us at the Urdu municipal school, where we went every morning. Class was from seven until one in the afternoon. At the beginning, I found it amusing to listen to the teacher, but I quickly got tired of it. I was like my father when he was a child. I had trouble concentrating. All I wanted to do was have fun. Whenever my father scolded me for not studying, I used to say, 'I'm just like you – I don't like school!' This always made him furious.

As soon as I saw an opportunity, I used to escape to go and join my mates in the streets. Sometimes, I didn't even go to school at all. But when I came home for lunch, my grandmother would know immediately from the mud on my uniform that I hadn't been in school. A dark blue strappy dress, white blouse, and ankle socks and black shoes are not exactly ideal for playing in the filth and dust.

'So you think that's an outfit for wrestling in the dust? And who is going to have to wash all that now?'

I used to have hair as long as my waist but my grandmother cut it short one day because it was so hot and I was always getting dirty. I felt sad. I loved my long hair! But my grandmother was good to me. She always defended me when the neighbours complained about my behaviour. I used to tell everyone to mind their own business, but everyone loves to gossip. Gossip is the best entertainment people have in the slums.

Dadi never yelled at me for long. Even if she tried to be strict, she spoiled me a lot. When I asked her to prepare my favourite dishes – chicken biryani or rice with curry and yoghurt, for example – she always gave in eventually. But she never failed to complain to Aba about my foolishness when he got home from work. And when he scolded me, he was truly angry! He wouldn't tolerate me getting dirty playing outside and missing school.

He even told me I wasn't allowed to play *kancha* (marbles). This is my favourite game. All the slum kids love this game. My aim is very good and I always win. We have a *kancha* battlefield, one of the few places that's quite flat and not littered with rubbish. All day long there are kids playing *kancha* here, and others waiting for their chance. We hit the target marble by using our middle finger. You have to get down on all fours to do this. Needless to say, it's impossible to stay clean for long. The children love this game as much as cricket, which is another popular slum game. But *kancha* is our game. Every kid has some marbles: big, small, multicoloured or sparkling ones. Trading marbles is a full-time job for slum kids.

'What have I just heard, Rubina? You skipped class again? You were seen playing *kancha* and eating rubbish near the tracks . . . '

'But I prefer playing!'

'That's enough of that!'

'Aba, Aba.'

'You have plenty of time to play after class. And

furthermore, that's no reason for getting your clothes filthy. Your grandmother has quite enough to do without having to put your foolishness right. How many times do I have to tell you to stop rolling about on the ground? It's dirty, and you're going to end up getting sick.'

'*Thik hai*. OK. It won't happen again.'

When he raises his voice, I feel very sad and I sulk in a corner until he comes to pacify me. He tickles my stomach, makes me jump in the air, and all is forgotten. He grumbles very loudly, but his anger doesn't last long. He has only slapped me once, when he saw me coming home with my feet covered with mud: I had gone out without my *chappals*. It's true that no one would walk barefoot in the slums. With the stagnant water, babies' pee and poo, people's spit, goat droppings and dog mess, and all the bits of scrap metal lying around, it's dangerous. I know that, but I was in such a hurry to see my friend's new dress. If anyone buys anything new in the slums, they have to flaunt it. I also love showing my things off to my friends. My possessions become more precious and beautiful when I see the light of jealousy in my friends' eyes.

Once a week, my father also sent us to the mosque to learn Arabic for 10 rupees a month. They put us in a room, girls on one side, boys on the other, and we read a prayer from the Koran out loud. For Aba it was important that we were able to read the holy book in Arabic. My father is quite religious and goes to the mosque every Friday; even when he has a lot of work, he always finds time to pray. At home, he has put up a photo of Ajmer Sharif, who's the patron saint of our family and hails from Rajasthan. Aba goes every July to meditate on his tomb; I went with him once. During my lessons at the mosque, I learnt many super-interesting things! Now I know that when a person dies, if he is a Muslim, he is put in a coffin, unlike the Hindus, who are cremated. And if you lie, God turns you into a lizard, and if you steal, you go straight to hell.

There was a girl of about fifteen who lived not far from me. One Friday after school, she went home and her mother, who was reading the Koran on the bed, said to her: 'Go wash your hands and then read the Koran with me.'

The girl was tired and didn't want to read the Koran. She started watching television and didn't listen to her mother.

'Watching television won't help you in life.'

The girl took no notice. Stretching out on the bed to watch the music videos, her leg hit the sacred book. A second later, her skin turned a strange colour and began to crack. Her face and body started

28

to change shape. In a few minutes, she'd become a lizard-woman. Her mother was shocked and scared. She started to shout and the whole neighbourhood was there. Doctors came but no one could treat her. They say her mother wanted to give her to a museum, but the daughter died a few days later. They even talked about it in the newspapers – it's no joke! This story gave me and many kids in the slums the creeps. I couldn't sleep for days after I heard it, and ever since I've been very careful to respect the Koran. And I never lie. Sometimes I lie, but very little lies, like when I need a few rupees from my father or have to get myself out of trouble.

'Aba, could you give me ten rupees?'

'What for?'

'I'd like to buy some masala chips.'

'Again?'

'I'm hungry.'

I mostly spend my days nibbling. Peanuts, biscuits, chocolates, spicy snacks, *kacha aam* (green mangoes) with a sprinkling of salt, or *paneer puris*, those delicious balls of fried batter filled with spicy potato stuffing. You can buy that for a few rupees on every corner of the slums. Then at mealtimes I'm not hungry, even when Dadi has cooked my favourite dish, chicken biryani. Sometimes, I completely forget lunch. When he doesn't see me come home, my father sends someone looking for me and he'll be waiting on the doorstep, shouting.

'Rubina, you must eat real meals. If you spend your time eating junk food, I won't give you any more money, do you understand?'

'Yes, Aba.'

Obviously, he forgets his threats as soon as he has made them, and as long as I ask nicely, he continues to slip me small bills regularly. He spoils me a lot and has trouble refusing me anything whatsoever as I have always been his favourite. Sana is very shy, very quiet, and doesn't ask for much. But I'm *bindass* (carefree) and I don't hold back. I just say what I want.

'Aba, can you give me five rupees?'

'Here, but that's it!'

'Thank you, Aba.'

Sana and I had a love-hate relationship. We fought and pulled each other's hair over small things like earrings and nail polish. She never wanted to share her things with me. Sana has always had her feet on the ground and I've always had my head in the sky. But we've always been protective of our little brother Abbas and we love him a lot. If anyone tries to mess with him, they've got me to answer to. I have never shied away from a fight. I think Abbas, my *chotu* (little one), is just like me.

Another of my pastimes in the slums is cycling. In Bandra East, a man named Salman who is the cousin of Azhar rents his bicycle at two rupees for five minutes. Depending on how much I have in my pocket, I go off for ten, fifteen or even thirty minutes. I love pedalling around in the slums, though it is quite a task to keep your balance between all the goats and vendors, especially while you're munching on peanuts or biscuits, which I keep in the basket on the handlebars. I often get cursed by the women and vendors on the ground if I run into their hens or their fruit and vegetables. In the slums, people shout at each other all the time. Men, women and even children keep abusing each other the whole day long.

When I'm not on the bike, I go and play in the street with my girlfriends, Rubina, Asa, Fana, Sohon and Luxhar. We're all the same age and I'm the gang leader. On the main street adjacent to the railway track is a makeshift stage, which is used for religious functions. My favourite is Nayaz, when for eleven days sermons are read out till late at night and after that really poor people are fed. It is an act of charity to get close to Allah. During this week, I stay out late with my friends and we pretend we're listening to the sermons. But we chat, giggle, push each other and pull each other's chairs. We get many glares from people but this just makes us laugh all the more.

For the rest of the time, this small wooden stage is our headquarters and meeting point. We put on little shows or just sit around chatting. I also love playing hide-and-seek with the other slum children: between the food stands, mountains of litter and alleyways full of secret nooks, there are so many amazing places to hide. In the evenings, we invite each other over to play games before dinner. Rubina, one of my closest friends, often used to come to my grandmother's, where we watched cartoons. I didn't like the days when our television broke down or someone pulled our cable wire to get channels for free, which meant we couldn't get a good picture. In the slums, people are always trying to get free electricity or cable. There are many fights over this, and sometimes they turn nasty.

I was lucky that my grandmother never asked me to help her in the house as I don't like doing house-work. With my father at work all day there was no one to supervise me. As a result, I was free as a bird to do as I chose. Unfortunately, everything I did eventually made it back to my father's ears.

'Rafiq, your daughter has gone and done it again.'

'What's she done now?'

'She hit my daughter. That's the second time this week.'

'*Acha*, I'm going to scold her.'

Aba didn't like it when I fought with my playmates. I wasn't particularly aggressive but I fought with girls or boys if they shouted at me or hit me. I don't take rubbish like that from anyone. The girl I hit started the fight by hitting me so I hit her back. Most often, it was for laughs. For example, I particularly like scaring people, including adults, by jumping on their back then holding on tight to their neck. The aim is to hang on as long as possible!

The times of year I love are the Muslim holidays, when people gather to enjoy festivities for three days. The festival of Id-ul-Zuha and Id-ul-Fitr is my favourite. There is an atmosphere of *mela* (carnival) in the slums. Distant relatives and cousins come to visit, and we organize meals that last for hours. The women start preparing food early in the morning and for once the slums have a nice aroma of biryani and chicken stew full of spices.

My father is very generous on these occasions. Last time he gave me more money than usual, bought me new clothes and also gave me a handbag to collect my Idi. For us it's a custom during Id for the elders to give money or gifts to the kids as a token of love. All the children get something. I love the way slums transform during Id: decorations, colourful lights, nice smells, no one fighting. The whole slum is one big happy family. My father also paid for my rides on the merry-go-round at the funfair that was set up in the neighbourhood during festival time, and bought us candies, ice creams and spicy snacks with a lot of *ilmi* (tamarind) in them. These were the only times I felt happy, content and normal, just like those people on the television screen.

2

I'm nine and I want to become an actress

Television is for sure the best thing that ever happened to me and to the people in the slums. I've been glued to this box for as long as I remember. With the coming of the cable, things got much more exciting and colourful. When I was young I just wanted to watch Mickey Mouse and other cartoons. I still love cartoons, especially Doremon and Pokémon. I watch them with my cousins and aunt regularly. Once, they stopped showing Doremon on television and my aunt was really sad.

'I don't like it when Doremon isn't on.'

She is such a kid! At home, we had an old telly and my big sister Sana and I always argued and fought over what to watch. Sana was obsessed with soap operas and missing a single episode was out of the question. If she did miss anything she'd go to her friend's house to find out what happened. The slums are addicted to *saas-bahu* soaps, which are all about mother-in-law and daughter-in-law relationships. I know women who plan their whole day according to the timing of their favourite soap. If I changed channels, Sana would shout at me. To make me let go of the remote control, she'd push me and pinch me, and I always ended up crying. And then I got older and I became a soap opera fan too, and then I started to dream about being part of this glittering, glamourous world.

I was fascinated by those beautiful women wearing jewels and nice make-up, and by their love stories as well as all the other complications in their lives. But movies have made the biggest impact on me. Those three hours make me forget everything. I love the singing and dancing and all the drama. I used to hoot and shout when the hero fought the bad guy, and then the happy ending would make me so happy. After watching a movie I always felt more certain that my life could have its own happy ending, with everything in place.

From time to time, my father took us to the Gaiety Galaxy, the big theatre in Bandra: a treat for everyone. We always bought tickets for the front-row seats as they don't cost much. You have to look up

36

to watch the film and you get a cricked neck. But I didn't mind that at all. In fact, I was lost in that big screen and the surround sound.

I especially like watching comedies, action and romantic movies. One of my favourite films is *Ghajini* with Aamir Khan and this very beautiful new actress called Asin. They are both so good-looking and the songs are really nice but not the kind you can dance to. Aamir Khan, who is one of the biggest Bollywood stars, plays the hero, who is very rich, whereas the heroine is very poor. They fall in love and are about to get married when a very bad man named Ghajini kills the woman and wounds the hero. After that the hero keeps forgetting things. He forgets everything as soon as it's happened, but he is still going to take revenge for the murder of his love. There are some very violent scenes, but I really liked the flashbacks that told the love story. It's magical, seeing a film on a large screen in a theatre. It feels like I'm part of the movie and it's all happening with me in it. I feel the same emotions: sad, happy, angry.

Salman Khan is my all-time favourite hero. Not only is he very good-looking but he has very big muscles. In every movie he has some scenes where he is bare chested and everyone loves that. All the boys in our slum want to have muscles like Salman Khan. He is very funny and his antics in the movies always crack me up. I have watched almost all his films. The last ones were *Yuvraj* and *Partner*. I especially liked the movie *Partner*; even his girlfriend Katrina Kaif is in it.

As for heroines, Preity Zinta is my idol. She is the biggest star in the world and very beautiful as well with her fair skin, and when she smiles she has dimples. I would like to be just like her when I grow up. The last movie I saw with Preity Zinta was *Krrish*, but she had a very small role. The story is about Krishna, a man born with superpowers, which he inherited from his father, who had been visited by an alien in a plane like a saucer when he was a child. To save the world, which is in danger because of one mad doctor, he becomes the superhero Krrish. The lead female role is played by Priyanka Chopra. I loved her latest movie too, called *Fashion*. It is about models and their lives. I didn't understand much of the storyline but the songs are very nice and me and my cousin Rukhsar know all the moves to the songs.

Me and my cousin Rukhsar spend entire afternoons imitating the choreographies of various movies. We take advantage of her parents' absence to rehearse the moves in front of the television, because it is very important for an actress to be a good dancer, and I love dancing as well. My cousin Rukhsar is a very good dancer and she has taught me many moves. For Rukhsar dancing is a passion, but she doesn't want to be an actress, and even if she did my uncle and aunt would never allow her. She is almost eighteen years old and girls of this age, according to my aunt, can't move freely in public alone, never mind go dancing. Almost all the girls in the slums get married when they are around eighteen. It is not too safe for grown-up girls here. The boys are really ill-mannered. They whistle at them, tease them and make dirty comments.

There are many children in the slums who dream of becoming a film star, but I knew I really would one day.

Three houses away from my aunt's shanty lives a man called Parvesh, a middle-aged man with oiled black hair, eyes lined with kohl and lips all red because he chews paan and masala all day. He doesn't speak much and is always spitting and leaving red trails behind him. He works for Pappu *bhai*, who is the biggest provider of juniors and extras in Bollywood. I have heard he has men everywhere out looking for different kinds of extras: fat people, small children, college students, even white-skinned people. Parvesh provides child extras, and he sometimes takes big boys for small roles and background appearances in movies. He has been in this industry for many years. He was a very good friend of my uncle. But now I know my uncle doesn't like him that much. He promised my uncle he would take my cousin Mohsin for an audition but he chose some other kids over him. Mohsin is a very good dancer and he is quite good-looking as well. But Parvesh is known to play these games, and no one dares say anything because everyone wants to be in his good books to get some work for their little ones.

Parvesh spotted me in the street when I was three. My father told me that he thought I was a very cute child. He offered me a role in a commercial, an awareness campaign for this disease called AIDS, with an actor called Suniel Shetty. I don't remember anything about my first appearance in front of the camera and they don't show this advertisement any more on television.

Parvesh met my father again around October 2007. This time he had a movie offer for me. When my father told me about it, I was jumping with joy. The role was small, but I'd be acting with stars and I couldn't imagine anything better than that. I went to the auditions, and I was selected. Unfortunately, the shooting was to take place on the same day as the wedding of a neighbour. I was really close to the bride. She was just like a sister to me and I wouldn't have missed the ceremony for anything in the world, even for a film. After all, she will get married only once, whereas I was certain I would have many other opportunities to act in a film. Still, I felt a little sad.

But I was right. Barely a month later, Parvesh stopped by the house again.

'*Namaste*, Rafiq.'

'*Namaste*, Parvesh. What brings you here?'

'I have a new offer for Rubina. It's an English film. Part of the shooting takes place in the slums of Mumbai, and the producers are looking for children familiar with this kind of environment.'

I was sitting there next to my father and hanging on to every word Parvesh was saying. I was thrilled: another movie offer. I was both restless and happy. This time, I wasn't going to miss it for anything. When my father turned to me, I couldn't stop smiling.

'*Karaegi, Rubina?* Will you do it?'

'Yes, please!'

'*Thik hai, thik hai!*'

After a few days Parvesh came by the house to pick me up. I didn't know what was going to happen or where I was going but I was super-excited. On the main road I saw a bus parked by the pavement along with many rickshaws. Inside, several dozen other children from the slums were already seated: some were friends, others looked familiar.

I asked Parvesh, 'Are they auditioning, too?'

41

'Yes, this is a huge foreign project. Five hundred children are going to take part in the audition, and I'm only in charge of about fifty of them from nearby slums. There are about fifteen of you coming from Bandra East.'

I had to compete against five hundred other children to get a role in this movie! The bus stopped in another slum not too far from ours and Parvesh escorted some more kids on to the bus, then we headed towards Andheri, one of Mumbai's largest suburbs. It took almost an hour to get there. This area houses some of the big Bollywood offices, Parvesh told us. We arrived at the India Take One production studio. I had never heard of them before. Inside, we were taken to a vast room filled with children, dozens and dozens of girls and boys about my age. I felt a bit lost so I stuck with the children from our slum. Everyone was excited and chatting but I was a bit distracted, wondering what they would make us do.

Parvesh told us, 'Get settled and wait here until you're called. If you're hungry or thirsty, help yourselves. There's everything you need on the table.'

I thought this would be a long audition with so many kids. But soon a woman came to speak to us. It took her a few minutes to silence everyone and get everyone's attention.

'Hello, children. My name is Loveleen and I'm the casting director. I know many of you don't speak English, so if you have questions, don't hesitate to come and ask me. For the audition, we're going to call you in groups of ten. When you hear your name, you will stand up and follow the person who comes to get you. Does everyone understand?'

There was a loud, 'Yeeees!'

When my turn came, I did as we'd been told. I was a bit nervous. In the audition room, Loveleen came over to us and explained: 'It's quite simple: you have to imagine you're running along a road. But mind you, this is not a race, so try not to push or shove anyone else.'

We looked at each other, a bit surprised. Usually in an audition they make us say dialogues and dance. So we were all just looking at each other, and then a boy asked Loveleen *didi*, '*Sirf bhagna hain?* We just have to run?'

'*Haan, sirf bhagna hain.* Yes, you just have to run. You start when I give you the signal. Are you ready?'

'Yes!'

'*Ek, do, teen – chalo!*'

The moment the signal was given we all started to run at the same time, in every direction, so it was a bit of a mess. We had barely run a few metres when we were told to stop.

'OK, that's fine! That was very good. Have a little rest then we'll start again. This time, you'll go a bit slower. But once again – this is not a race and we don't care who is the fastest. We just want to see you run.'

I kept thinking about what kind of movie it could be and different themes were running through my head: action, sports, suspense.

They made us run three times, and then we went to the other room and sat and waited with the other children. When everyone had had their turn, Loveleen came to speak to us again.

'That was perfect. Thank you very much, children. I'll see you tomorrow for the next part of the auditions.'

And that was it for the day. It wasn't that difficult! Parvesh had warned us that the auditions would be spread out over several days. We were all pretty excited at the idea of coming back and I had made a few new friends as well. So it was not just an audition for me, but also a bit of an outing.

The bus dropped us all off in our slums. When I got home, my little brother, Abbas, was waiting, eager to know what I'd done.

'So, how was it? What did you have to do?'

'I ran.'

'What do you mean?'

'I'm saying I just ran – that's all. I think it's a film about running.'

Abbas wasn't that happy with my answer but he still rushed out to tell his friends and to have a good laugh about it.

The next day, at the same time, the bus was waiting for us at the entrance to the slum again. Inside, I saw all the kids from the day before. Great! We had all passed the running audition. When we arrived at the studio, Loveleen, who was very sweet, was waiting for us.

'Good morning, children. How are you? Not too tired?'

'No!'

'Good. Today will be like yesterday. You'll each be called in; the difference is that there are going to be smaller groups of three or four. And this time, you're going to have a few lines to say. It's not difficult – you'll only have to learn them by heart just beforehand.'

So, I thought, we will have something to say at last. I was glad to know that English movies also had dialogue.

When my turn came, I was told to sit at a large wooden table with three other kids. Each of us had an empty plate in front of us. Loveleen quickly explained the scene.

'OK, children, you're going to be served some *dal* and *chawal* and you're going to eat. Just remember to eat like you haven't had a real meal for a long time.'

This was going to be easy! I was feeling hungry anyway.

'Rubina, after you've eaten a few mouthfuls, you'll have to say: "If the man fills our plate a second time that will mean he's really nice!" OK?'

'OK.'

We did this scene again and again so that everyone had their chance to say this line. The next day, I returned to the set, and the following days, too, each time with new lines to deliver. Sometimes we saw Loveleen quickly translating a scene from English into Hindi in a corner of the studio before having us act it out. As soon as it was my turn, I would forget everything around me. We still didn't know what this movie was all about, but I took my part and my lines very seriously. It wasn't hard. It felt as if I had been doing it all my life.

The atmosphere was relaxed, and everyone was very nice to us. I made many new friends. As the days went by, fewer and fewer kids joined us on the bus each morning. I was happy still to be in the running and I was getting very used to the auditions.

I met Azharrudin. I had seen him before roaming in the slums but we weren't friends until the auditions. Everyone called him Azhar. He is a year older than me and also lives in Bandra East, on the other side of the road. His house is just a few tin sheets with a yellow plastic sheet for a roof. With him, I never stopped laughing. He always played the clown, cracking jokes, making funny faces or imitating other children. It was so much fun.

I'd been going to the auditions for more than ten days but I still didn't know whether I'd been selected. Every time Parvesh came he brought some exciting news for me, so when he came by one afternoon I wanted to know what was the latest. He told me to get ready to meet the director of the movie. I bombarded him with questions but he hushed me by saying that I had to get ready. Later I met him at the main road where he was waiting with Azhar. We took a bus to Juhu Beach. It takes half an hour to reach Juhu from our slum and I was excited about seeing the beach. I had seen it in the movies and heard about it from friends but I'd never been there. We passed some very big houses just like the ones in the soaps, and there were also nice hotels and restaurants. Finally we turned off and I saw this huge stretch of beach. It was full of people, some standing, some paddling in the water, and vendors were selling snacks, gola and candies. I wanted to get close to the water and I looked at Parvesh pleadingly to stop just for a few minutes but he refused because we were running late. I had my eyes fixed on the water till we took another turn-off. The bus dropped us on the main crossing and it took us another ten minutes on foot to reach this huge hotel called Sun and Sand. It was very close to the beach.

'Just one minute?'

'No, let's go.'

We had arrived in front of a very big door. I didn't know places like this existed and I wanted to explore. The porter saluted us as if we were important people. We stepped inside and it was so *thanda* (cool). Azhar said the whole place had air-conditioning. Everything was incredibly clean. You could see your own shadow on the shiny floor. There were shops on the right-hand side selling things like chocolates, creams, and beautiful necklaces and rings.

'Have a seat on the sofa. I'll be right back.'

Sit down? No way! We had only one desire and that was to see everything. It's not every day you get to go to a place like this. We were about to explore the pretty terrace with a view of the beach when Parvesh came back to get me.

'*Chalo*, let's go. They're waiting for us.'

I followed him down a long corridor, which had

many doors with numbers on them. We stopped in front of one of them and Parvesh knocked timidly.

'Come in!'

Inside the room, Loveleen was waiting for us, smiling but looking serious. During the auditions, I hadn't had much chance to talk her. I didn't know she'd be here today but seeing her familiar face gave me some confidence. She stood up to greet us and then she took me by the shoulders and steered me in front of a very gentle-looking man wearing glasses. By his white and pink skin, I figured he wasn't from Mumbai, and maybe not even India.

'Danny, this is Rubina. Rubina, let me introduce Danny Boyle, the director of the film.'

'*Namaste.*'

'*Namaste.*'

I'd seen foreigners in movies but this was the first time I'd ever talked to one in real life. I stared curiously at this man with a high forehead and a big smile. I didn't speak a word of English, and he didn't speak a word of Hindi except *namaste*. But he looked relaxed and nice, and I felt comfortable with him. He said a few words, smiling, and Loveleen translated.

'Danny wants you to enact the scene in the rain.'

'*Thik hai!* OK!'

I had already rehearsed this rain scene with Azhar and Ayush, another boy our age, during the auditions.

I was supposed to act as if it was raining, and I had to stand in front of Azhar and Ayush looking helpless and trying to convince them to let me in their shelter. During the auditions, Azhar had laughed a lot at the pleading look on my face. So I stood in the middle of the room, hunched my shoulders as if trying to protect myself against a heavy downpour, and looked as unhappy as possible.

Danny stood up and spoke. He sounded enthusiastic. Loveleen translated for me.

'Danny is really delighted and says you've done a great job.'

I was happy with my performance. Loveleen and Parvesh exchanged a few words, then Danny said, 'Bye bye, Rubina,' and we left the room. Back in the lobby my eyes were pulled back to that terrace outside and I asked Parvesh permission to go and have a look. He answered, laughing, *'Thik hai!'*

Outside, there was a swimming pool with many foreigners either sleeping on the wooden beds around it or swimming in the water. I had never seen a swimming pool before. It was so clean and the water was the colour of the sky but a bit darker. There was also another small swimming pool with some bubbles coming in from all sides. The people were wearing very small clothes, like underwear. I didn't know that adults could go around in a public place in their undergarments. No one in my slum dressed like that. But I was fascinated by the water, and I could see the beach from there as well. As far as my eyes could see there was nothing but water.

I love water! I went over to the edge of the pool, dying to dive in. I took off my *chappals* and touched the water with my feet, but then Parvesh rushed over to me.

'Rubina, what are you doing?'

'I want to go for a swim!'

'I'm sorry, but that's just not possible. You have to have a bathing costume to go in the pool.'

When I bathe in the tank next to the house in my slum, I go in fully dressed. I was so disappointed, but there was nothing I could do.

We took a bus back to our slum, and although I was a bit upset and angry about not being able to swim I was also really excited to tell my brother and friends about what I'd seen. On the way, Parvesh seemed more at ease. He had some news for me. He told me I'd been selected for the movie.

'*Sach mein?* Really?'

'*Hain.*'

'*Acha!*'

I had no idea what the film was about and I didn't even know what role I'd got, but that didn't matter. All I knew was that I, Rubina, was going to make a film, a real one! I couldn't wait to tell Aba. Back in Bandra, as soon as I got off the bus, I ran along the railway. I ran into people who cursed me and I also stepped into the muck but I didn't care. I was going to be in a movie! Parvesh came running after me. My father, who was waiting on the doorstep, wanted to know what all the excitement was about. I could hardly get the words out so he told me to sit down and catch my breath. Finally, I gasped, 'Aba! Aba! I'm going to be in a film!'

'Whoa! Calm down, Rubina!'

'A film, Aba, can you believe it?'

I was going crazy with happiness. I got up again and started dancing all round him. By this time Parvesh had come in with a smile on his lips, which is something you don't see very often. Aba gave him a questioning look.

'Congratulations, Rafiq *bhai*. Rubina has been selected from among five hundred children!'

I was sure my father was proud of me, but he was a bit hesitant. He asked Parvesh some questions.

'So what is this film?'

'An English film.'

The film wasn't going to be shown on Indian screens. For me, that didn't matter: a film was a film, and whether it was foreign-made or local it changed nothing. The main thing was that I was in it and that

I was now an actress.

'And what's it about?'

'It is a story about children living in slums.'

'How long will the filming last?'

'Only four days – five at the most. I'll be back to pick up Rubina within the week.'

Parvesh and Aba spoke about money, but I knew it didn't count: I was so happy that my father would have accepted even if he had been offered only 100 rupees. In any event, Aba knew nothing about the film industry and how it works and how important my role would be, and neither did I. So we had little option but to take on trust everything Parvesh said.

Bursting with excitement, I asked, 'What's my part?'

'Your part is that of a poor little girl. It's not the main role but it's an important one. You'll see: a large number of actors have been recruited for this film, but only three children were chosen. Azhar is also selected.'

Azhar? Well, I know him a bit now, but he doesn't look much like hero material. Before Parvesh left, I wanted to know the name of the movie so I could flaunt it in front of my friends. I was going to be a star in a foreign film! I asked him, *Picture ka naam kya hain?*

'Slumdog Millionaire.'

'*Salim Daag Milli Nair*? What a funny title!'

I didn't know what it meant, but it didn't matter. I was just thrilled that I was going to be in front of a camera with people treating me like a star.

'Lights, camera, action!' And I was so totally ready to enter the world of my dreams.

3

Action!

Filming started in December 2007. It was a very hot day and we took a bus with Parvesh, and Azhar and his mother. We were taken to the same place where the auditions were held. Loveleen and Danny would be waiting for us. When we reached the studio, we met another boy, named Ayush, who was also our age but he came from the suburbs of Mumbai. His father wasn't poor and he didn't come from the slums. The only thing we knew about the movie was that it was about slum kids, but we had no idea about which roles we'd been chosen to play. Loveleen took us round the studio, showing us where to find the food stalls, the toilets and the rest area. They all were treating us with so much respect, like we were important people. Then she explained what they wanted us to do.

'So, in this film there are going to be three main characters: Jamal, who's the hero, his brother Salim, and the heroine will be Latika. You three are going to play these characters when they were children. Ayush, you're Jamal. Azhar, you're playing Salim. And Rubina, you're Latika. Do you all understand?'

'Yes, yes, got that.'

'The scenes will be easy – you've already rehearsed a lot of them during the auditions. We'll ask you to do the same things again, but this time there'll be a camera there too. *Thik hain?*'

OK? It was more than OK! The three of us couldn't wait to get started. We were introduced to a few other people. I particularly liked Natasha, the make-up artist. I wanted to be friends with her. She could teach me all about doing a perfect face just like in the movies. She was very helpful, and so was Loveleen, who was always around, trying to make sure we were comfortable.

'If you have any questions or if you need anything at all, just come and ask me.'

'What are we going to do first?'

'First of all we're going to do some camera tests, and then we'll start with a very happy scene. Rubina and Ayush, you have to show that you are very close. It's the start of a very pure and beautiful love that will bind you together for life, although you don't know that yet.'

The start of a very pure love. I didn't understand what she meant, but at least it wasn't about being in love with Azhar. That would have been almost impossible! But I was excited and wanted to explore. I'd never been to a studio before. There were so many people busy checking lights, struggling with wires or running around waving their arms and talking loudly. When I found myself standing in the middle of the set, with dozens of cameras and lights around me, I felt a bit nervous and scared – until Danny uncle said, 'Action!' Then everything seemed to fade away in the background. It didn't bother me that so many people were watching me. When I wasn't in a scene I watched Ayush and Azhar. That was when I started to realize that even though they had important roles, I was the heroine of the movie. It wasn't long before the three of us were best friends. Between takes, we'd run around asking the cameramen questions and chasing each other in and out of the sets. We were curious and wanted to know about everything, from wires and lights to make-up brushes. It was great fun on set and everyone was really nice to us. People kept asking, 'Do you need anything? Would you like something to eat?'

I've never drunk so many bottles of Coca-Cola or eaten so many ice creams in my life. I spent a lot of time with Natasha. She'd show me her make-up and let me try things out. She had so many things: many colours of lipstick, things to put on cheeks and eyelids.

Whenever Danny had five minutes free, he'd come and play with us. I used to like the hand game, where he'd put his hands out, palms down, and I had to try to hit them before he pulled them away. In the end we always burst out laughing. When we had to shoot a scene, Loveleen always carefully explained it to us before we started. Actually it was very easy. We'd rehearsed the scenes over and over again during the auditions. No one screamed at us when we forgot our lines or started giggling halfway through a dialogue, and Danny always tried to make sure we were at ease.

'Are you feeling tired? Do you want to have a little rest before we carry on?'

Sometimes it was a bit hard and tiring. Like the scene with the rain – that was a lot less fun than in the rehearsals. There was a kind of machine hidden behind the set from which water came out fast and continuously just like real rain, and I got completely soaked! The day we shot that scene it was late and I was already very tired. Ayush and Azhar had taken shelter in an abandoned shack. In the film I had to stand out in the open, a little way away from them, without moving. Then I had to crouch down and draw patterns in the mud with a bit of wood with rain falling over me, looking miserable, until they made some space for me in the shelter. When I felt the first drops landing on my head I got a real surprise – the water was freezing! Then the drops turned into a really heavy downpour, like monsoon rains. It was coming down so hard I had to struggle to keep my eyes open.

'Cut!'

When I heard that I ran over to the assistants, who immediately wrapped me up in a big towel to get me dry. Azhar and Ayush were still sitting comfortably in their hut, laughing at my dripping face. I thought it was all over, but then Loveleen said, 'That was very good, Rubina, but we're going to do it again, OK?'

Oh no! I could've done without that! Even though cold water was pouring down on me I was still having trouble staying awake. My eyes kept closing and I just wanted to go to sleep. We did that scene over and over. I was feeling very cold. Whenever Danny uncle shouted 'Cut!' I would run over to a little electric heater they'd put next to the set. Then, when I was holding out my hands in the hot air and just starting to unfreeze, I'd hear Danny uncle shout:

'That was really good! OK . . . let's do it again!'

After a while I could understand a few words of English and I knew what he meant. I'd pretend not to understand so I could stay by the heater a little longer, then I'd go back. That was the most difficult scene of the whole shoot. And once, someone was closing the toilet door and my finger got in the way. But there was a doctor on the set who bandaged it. In the slums, kids keep falling and getting hurt so it didn't bother me that much. The other scenes were much easier. Me, Ayush and Azhar were particularly good at doing the external scenes in Dharavi. Dharavi is spread out over a huge area, with many, many people and workshops. It's quite easy to get lost there. When they asked us to run through the narrow alleyways, the cameras had trouble keeping up. Dancing barefoot in the middle of a dirty puddle and running between cows and people in a narrow lane was just what we were used to. It was like playing hide-and-seek outside our own homes – except that we had to keep doing the same things over and over and over until Danny uncle was happy with the take.

Really, the things they wanted us to act were

just everyday life to us. Rubbish full of rats and cockroaches, little shacks and open drains everywhere – that's how we lived. Unlike the hero of the film, I've never collected rubbish, but Azhar had done it to make a few rupees. And the public toilets Danny uncle showed in the film, the little wooden huts raised on sticks over disgusting filth, well, they were really there in Dharavi. The scene where Jamal gets locked in the toilets by his brother Salim and escapes through a hole dug in the ground was one of the funniest scenes we shot. According to the scene, Ayush (Jamal) was ready to do absolutely anything to get the autograph of the film star Amitabh Bachchan, his great idol, even if it meant jumping into toilet waste. When Loveleen briefed Ayush about this, he didn't go along with it at all. No way was he going to jump in to a pile of poo! Me and Azhar thought it was hilarious. We had a good laugh when we heard what he had to do. We were pretty happy that we didn't have to do a scene like that. But Loveleen quickly told him not to worry.

'Don't panic, Ayush! Want to know exactly what you're going to land in?' She looked at us and we were still laughing at Ayush's bad luck.

'Yes . . .'

'Chocolate!'

'Really?'

'Yes, litres of chocolate!'

At first Ayush didn't believe it. Then he got really excited. In fact, we were all licking our lips. All of a sudden me and Azhar went quiet. Now we wanted to have a scene like this!

You should have seen them getting the mixture ready on set. The assistants poured kilos and kilos of chocolate in to a big pot, with butter and mint, then mixed it all up for hours over a low heat. The whole studio had this sweet, yummy chocolatey smell and I just wanted to jump right in and eat the whole lot. In the slums, I do get to eat sweets, but mostly they are fruit flavour and some chocolate candies. This mixture looked and smelled so nice I couldn't help but stare at it and hang around next to the pot. It was making my mouth water!

When the mixture was ready, we begged Danny to let us taste it. He saw the looks on our faces and agreed at once.

'Come on, it's my round! Everyone can have some!'

We ran towards the pot, screaming. Everyone came over to get a bowlful. Mmm! It was delicious. Even Danny liked it. I saw him licking his fingers before getting back to work.

'Right, ready everyone! We can't let it get cold!'

I would have given anything to be Ayush just

then. Ayush kept looking at us, all happy that he was going to fall into that yummy chocolate. We found a good place in a corner to watch the scene so we wouldn't miss a thing. Ayush was waiting, crouching over the hole. He was having trouble keeping a straight face.

'Camera!'

Ayush looked down through the hole that did the job of a toilet bowl, and then he looked a bit hesitant, but it was something he had to do to get his favourite star's autograph. He started to pinch his nostrils, as he'd been asked to do. When we saw Ayush holding his nose, Azhar and I started laughing so hard. Then Ayush began making terrible faces and we had to struggle to keep quiet. The scene was complicated to do and everyone – including Ayush, of course – knew it was supposed to be done in just one take. If they had to do it again because of our noisy laughing, Danny would be really angry. Azhar and I put our hands over our mouths so no one would hear us. At last Ayush jumped right in, splashing chocolate all over the cameras.

My stomach was hurting and I was having difficulty breathing, we were laughing so much. My hand stayed tight over my mouth until Danny shouted 'Cut!' and then Azhar and I exploded into loud mad laughter. We just couldn't stop. Ayush stood there with that chocolatey liquid dripping off him, waiting to be told what to do and not daring to move. That made us laugh even harder. In the end Danny said, 'Good, that's great!' Ayush was relieved. He started licking himself like a little cat. He offered us some, but . . . eeurgh! That's my funniest memory from the shoot. I still laugh whenever I think of that day. When I saw this scene on the screen it looked so real!

By now we had been filming for nearly two weeks. Danny had soon realized that five days wasn't going to be enough for all the scenes we were in. Shooting in the slums had turned out to be more complicated than they thought as there were so many people surrounding the camera. The heat made everything take longer too, because they had to cool the cameras down several times during the day using bags of ice. All this meant that, even though we were there from morning till night, we could never film for more than two or three hours a day.

Strangely, one of the best scenes, and my father's favourite, was the one with the train. It sounded so simple: the three heroes, Jamal, Salim and Latika, are running away from a horrible orphanage where the man in charge wanted to make them handicapped and send them out to beg, which is what happens to the other children in the orphanage. The bad guys are chasing them so they run along the railway tracks, trying to jump on to a moving train. Jamal and Salim manage to get on, but Latika is slower than the boys and she doesn't make it. She manages to grab Salim's hand, but at the last moment he lets go. The train they used for the filming was a real one. When I saw it I was really scared. It wasn't the idea of running along the train that frightened me, but the idea of holding the hand of someone who was on board. What if I slipped and fell?

Loveleen tried to reassure me. 'Don't worry. The train will be going very slowly. Nothing bad can possibly happen to you. There are many people here to make sure that you don't get hurt. You just have to run quite fast and concentrate on what you're doing.'

Danny talked to us for a long time before we had to play the scene, making sure we all understood exactly what to do. It was a bit more complicated for Ayush and Azhar. They had to actually climb on to the train. Azhar just wanted to get on with it as quickly as possible; he thought it was all great fun. When he saw that I was frightened, he started teasing me.

'Chapati-face, are you scared of trains?'

It was always like that. Azhar never missed a chance to clown around. Usually we both managed to have a good time, but sometimes he couldn't help teasing me just for the pleasure of seeing me get annoyed.

'Hey, monkey-face, you're going to mess it all up!'

The stupid names he called me started to drive me crazy. Azhar's mother never told her son off. She was there every day, but she never said a word. She just sat there drinking cup after cup of chai the whole day. Danny sometimes told Azhar to behave when he messed about on set, but he never shouted at him.

'Calm down, Azhar. You can mess about when we've got the shot.'

In my view a bit of shouting wouldn't have done Azhar any harm. But I always gave a good fight if he picked on me.

This train scene was just like the ones they have in Bollywood movies. I was lucky with the scene – it only took one take. It turned out that running along a train was easier than I thought. But running with *chappals* was a bit uncomfortable. I was totally out of breath by the end, which gave Azhar something else to tease me about.

But I took my revenge with the *mirchi* (chilli) scene. It was to teach a lesson to Salim (Azhar), who bullies everyone and threatens to drop the baby in the movie. Latika – in other words, me – had her revenge, both in the movie and in real life.

The idea of putting *mirchi* on his willy made Azhar a bit quieter than usual. While the assistants were getting the scene ready, Ayush and I teased him mercilessly.

'Chilli inside Azhar's pants!'

'Hey, Azhar, you like hot food? Fancy a bit of chilli?'

Everyone was laughing except Azhar, who kept on complaining and asking Loveleen, 'Are you sure those chillies aren't too hot?'

'It's all right, Azhar, we've picked very mild chillies. You'll hardly feel a thing, honest.'

At last everyone was in their places. The other child extras lay down on mats, all close together. Azhar lay down in the middle, looking rather worried.

'Quiet please, camera's rolling!'

Everyone had to pretend to be asleep, but a few were still giggling.

'Sshh, children, no messing about, the camera's rolling, I said!'

We all found it hard to be serious. Even Azhar couldn't help giggling. It took a while before it was completely silent. In the scene Latika gets up, tiptoes over to Salim's mat, carefully slips the little red chillies in to his pants and quickly goes back to her place to wait for the burning to wake Salim up. While I was doing all this, I had to act very *chalo* (clever), then burst out laughing when Salim started to yell. It goes without saying that I didn't have to pretend, and the others didn't either. When Azhar jumps off his bed shouting with pain, all the children wake up and start to laugh and point at him. Azhar drops his pants and runs like crazy towards the bathroom, grabs the water pipe and tries to cool himself down between his legs, while all the other actors laugh and shout, 'Chillies on his willy! Chillies on his willy!'

It was in the script to laugh but we didn't have to act. We all laughed till we cried. And I must say Azhar acted being in pain brilliantly. You should have seen the faces he was pulling, with his mouth wide open and his eyes rolling about. It was so funny to see him naked and I still haven't stopped teasing him about it.

Finally we had a dance sequence, and all my practice with Rukhsar came in handy. I loved dancing on the 'Ringa Ringa' song. I had to sing and dance on the railway track. I fell in love with the song the very first time I heard it, and after listening to it a few times I even knew the words. Danny did a lot of takes as he needed different angles. But I didn't mind – the opposite, in fact. I could have gone on doing it for ever. I was singing and dancing to the song just like a Bollywood actress. I was thrilled to have a song in the movie at last. I was thinking that even the audience will sway as they are listening to this song and looking at me.

I'd been imitating actresses for so long and now I had a song of my own. That evening when I went home, I rushed to my cousin's place to show her the moves. Rukhsar was as excited as me. She came and stood next to me at once to copy the steps. My uncle and aunt laughed as they watched us dancing in the middle of the room. Ten days later we shot the film's final song, 'Jai Ho', at Victoria Station. So I had two songs to my credit. My cousins were fast to learn my new dance steps. We did spend a lot of evenings doing them.

Every night when I got back from filming, I'd tell my family the story of that day's scene. My little brother Abbas really enjoyed the one with the chillies. Just the thought of having his trousers full of *mirchi* made him go crazy laughing. He thought it was a really good prank to play on slum kids. And Aba couldn't believe that I did the train scene in just one take. But what impressed them most was when I told them I'd met Anil Kapoor. He's a superstar in India, he's made dozens of films, and I've seen loads of them, in the cinema and on television. Now at last they were all convinced that I really was acting in a big movie.

In the film his role is that of Prem, the host of *Kaun Banega Crorepati?* (*Who Wants to be a Millionaire?*). As the filming took longer than expected, Danny started working with the adult actors while we kids were still around. Sometimes we'd meet older Jamal and Latika, who were played by Dev Patel and Frieda Pinto. Me, Ayush and Azhar used to observe the way they acted. And that was how I saw Anil Kapoor in the flesh for the first time. The set of the TV game show had been put together with seats for the pretend audience. But when the cameras were focusing just on the middle of the set, anyone could go and sit there to watch. It wasn't just me – everybody wanted to see Anil Kapoor. But he didn't know me. To him, I was just another extra. He didn't yet know that I also had an important role to play. That day I didn't get an opportunity to ask for his autograph, but I hoped I'd get another chance. Just seeing him was really amazing. Back home everyone kept pestering me with questions.

'Anil Kapoor, how does he look?'

'Does he look good?'

'Rubina, did you speak to Anil Kapoor?'

My father and uncles were particularly impressed. They have grown up watching his movies. One of

70

my father's favourites is *Mr India*, where Anil Kapoor gets a gadget that makes him invisible.

'You're certainly meeting great people. You seem to be living the life of a real star!'

I also really liked Frieda Pinto and Dev Patel. Frieda *didi* was really nice to us. We joked together, and I particularly liked watching her get ready for her scenes.

It was true. Filming was like a dream and I never wanted it to stop. There wasn't a single day that wasn't amazing fun. After we'd all been working together for a long time, Danny called us all in to talk to us. Loveleen translated.

'The shooting is over, children; we've got everything we wanted. I've got to concentrate on the grown-ups now. Thank you, you've been wonderful!'

I knew this was going to happen, but I hoped it wouldn't happen that soon. For a month, we'd put everything into this film. We'd got used to life on the set. It was weird to think of leaving Danny, Loveleen, Natasha and the rest of the crew. Everyone had been so kind and nice to us. I couldn't help feeling incredibly sad at the idea of leaving it all behind. I would really miss being in front of the camera and being treated like a star.

'Don't look so sad! Don't you want to see yourselves on the big screen?'

'Yes!'

'You wait and see – you'll be amazed!'

'Hum kab milege?'

'Of course we'll all see each other again! We haven't finished shooting the film yet, and then I'm going to stay in India a bit longer. I promise we'll see each other a lot.'

It was hard being back in the slums. Things weren't the same. I missed eating ice cream and chocolates and drinking cold drinks. The people at the studio were really nice. For the first few days I found it hard to adjust. Then Parvesh turned up.

'Danny wants to see you. I think he's got a surprise for you.'

I was thrilled that I'd be seeing my friends and Danny uncle again. And there was going to be a surprise too! I was wondering what it could be. We went again to the India Take One office and were greeted by Santa Claus. I'd only seen Santa on the television before. It was 24 December and one of the technicians had dressed up for us. At home we didn't celebrate Christmas, it was just an ordinary day. Me, Ayush and Azhar got given presents of sweets and toys by Santa. And then, for Happy New Year, we were called by Danny uncle to his office and given more presents. I love playing with Danny uncle. I love the way he smiles all the time. I got some toys from him that you can use to make mountains on a beach, and some glow-in-the-dark stickers. I was so happy that Danny uncle hadn't forgotten us and that we mattered to him.

4

'In Bollywood, you'll never make it big if you only speak Hindi. If you want to get on in this business, you have to learn English.'

When the filming of *Slumdog Millionaire* was over, life went back to normal, but I felt more confident and hopeful about my future. Right from the start, Danny uncle had told us that we needed to go to school. Everyone else on the set talked about how important education was. For Danny uncle it was the most important thing, our only chance of getting out of the slums and having a better life. No one at home spoke English except for my cousin, Rukhsar. My father wanted us to learn Urdu, the language of the Koran, instead, and English schools are much more expensive and we didn't have any next to our slum. So it was something I could never think of. Before the shooting of *Slumdog*, I never felt bad about not knowing English. But when I was on set and I heard everyone talking in English, I wanted to be part of it. I knew Danny uncle was right. If I wanted to be an actress, speaking English and having a good education were important.

In films I can see that people talk very well and have good manners. They don't call each other names or shout. It must be because they've all had such a good education. I've never heard of any actor coming from the slums either. Azhar also knew that if we wanted to be actors we had a lot of things to learn. We would have to work to improve ourselves if we wanted to make it big.

Danny uncle had promised he would enrol us in an English-speaking school as soon as the filming was over, and he kept his promise. Around early March, he and Loveleen visited Aseema School to enrol me and Azhar. I had heard that the Aseema School was an English-medium school for underprivileged children, a school with a very good reputation that was extremely difficult to get into. Danny went to visit the school on its annual open day. He met the teachers, found out about the education they provided and persuaded the principal to take us. Danny took care of all the formalities on behalf of my father.

The school provided us with navy blue uniforms and with books as well. I was ecstatic to have new books with crisp white pages and everything written in English. Danny uncle even hired a rickshaw to come and pick us up every day and bring us back home after school in the evening. That rickshaw cost 1,500 rupees, but I don't think that was much for Danny.

And Loveleen said to my father, 'Danny's assistant, Maxima, will call you regularly to see if you need anything.'

Unlike Urdu school, the classes at Aseema were in the afternoon. Early in June, at 1 p.m. sharp, a rickshaw arrived outside the slum to take us to school. It was a ten-minute ride. At Urdu school I used to be in class four, but at Aseema, because I had very poor English, they put me back to class one, just above kindergarten level. I was both excited and nervous. I was with Azhar and we were the oldest in our class of around fifty children. When the others heard we'd been in a film, their attitude towards us immediately changed. A lot of them came and asked us questions. They wanted to know if it was hard acting in front of a camera, what the film was about and, most of all, if we'd met any film stars. We soon made lots of friends and it wasn't too difficult to adapt.

Azhar can never keep his mouth shut, even during

class, but I concentrated on my work. I didn't chat much with the other children during the lessons. I hated maths and I loved English, but I worked hard at everything. I wanted to learn as fast as possible how to talk like an adult, and how to be polite and well-mannered. And I was happy going to school because I made many good friends. We played, chatted and spoke about our families in the breaks. I learned something new every day. I used to go home and repeat the new English words I'd learned to my cousins and to Sana and Abbas.

'Good night, sweet dreams.'

Soon my hard work in class started to get noticed. My teacher, Sumatra, was pleased with my behaviour and progress and she made me the class monitor. Whenever she went out of the room, I would take her place and keep an eye on the class. I was even allowed to punish children who disturbed the others or didn't do as I said. I took my role very seriously and thought of myself as no less than a teacher at those times.

Nobody minded – except Azhar, of course, who wasn't going to miss any chance to make fun of me. Azhar and I were not such good friends any more, not since we'd finished filming. I sometimes bumped into him in the slums, but I'd keep my distance.

It was not just my good behaviour that earned me

the role of class monitor. My results were really good too. I got As in almost everything. I got almost full marks in English and maths. I was sure that Danny uncle would be proud of me. Azhar only got Bs. I'm so pleased I got better results than him.

I hadn't forgotten the way he'd teased me during the shoot and now I had to tolerate him at school too. Of course, he went on calling me all kinds of stupid animal names, like *bandar* (monkey). In the playground, he was always getting in to fights with the other boys too. His favourite trick was to copy me, to repeat everything I said, like a parrot. This made me so angry sometimes I wanted to hit him.

'Sit down.'

'Sit down.'

'Shut up, Azhar!'

'Shut up, Azhar!'

He was so annoying! Luckily there was a girl called Anjali who was as old as me. We became best friends and were always together. In fact, the teacher was worried about us copying each other's work, so during tests we had to sit apart. But it didn't matter, because we spent all the rest of the time together, playing, skipping or just chatting.

Every now and then Maxima would call me and my father to see how things were going at school and whether I needed anything. Apart from this, filming was now all in the past for us. Around the end of August, Maxima called and told us that *Slumdog Millionaire* had been released in the USA. At that time, we didn't know the film was going to come out in India too, and so we weren't sure we'd ever see it on the big screen. Every now and then we'd sing 'Jai Ho' or 'Ringa Ringa' with my cousin Rukhsar, who had learned all the moves by heart and even taught it to our two little brothers, Abbas and Mohsin. My cousin, Mohsin, now was eager to do some auditions and be part of a film too, and then to go on to study medicine.

Life was more or less normal: playing with friends and hanging out in the slums. Things were not that great at home. My father was recovering from a bad fall and was out of work. He'd broken his ankle falling down the stairs on the bridge over the railway tracks near our house. Some neighbours helped him and brought him to my grandmother's place. He was in terrible pain and his face was red. It made me so sad to see him like that and I couldn't stop crying. He had a series of operations that used up most of the 40,000 rupees I'd made from my role in Danny uncle's film. My father got better, but his ankle was still not fully healed. There was no way he could go back to work as a carpenter. Before, he'd made 100–200 rupees a day on the building sites, which was just enough to pay for our food. Sometimes he earned a bit more, which was used to pay for *bijli* (electricity) and other expenses. You can't live without *bijli* in the slums because there are no windows for air to come in and it gets hard to breathe. Before, when we didn't have our own electricity connection, we used to plug our wire in at a neighbour's place for a few rupees.

It was becoming difficult to make ends meet at home. There are six people to feed in our house: me, my grandmother, my sister, my brother, my father and his brother, Uncle Gulam, who was two years older than my father. He had a tea stall, but since he'd started drinking he'd stopped going there. Aba had no work so he took it over, which brought in enough just to survive. We ate simple food like *dal* and *chawal* (rice); meat was a delicacy. My grandmother was always complaining that the price of things kept going up. Mutton and chicken became really expensive, going from 40 to 100 rupees a kilo, which meant less biryani for me. For Aba, who'd always provided everything for us, it was a very hard time.

My father met Munni just before I started the English school. She was a Muslim like him, two years younger at thirty-four. When her first husband left her a long time ago, she moved with her three children from Kolkata to Mumbai. Munni came to Mumbai like many other people in the hope that it would be easier to find work. There are many people in the slums who left their village and moved to Mumbai to make a better life for themselves. Every day I see neighbours' relatives coming to stay with them to look for a job. Every year, there are more and more people in the slums. My grandmother says that people think Mumbai is a land of dreams. I wonder how many fulfil their dreams. But I'm happy that my *kismat* (fate) is better than others'.

Munni had been living in our neighbourhood for several years, just near my uncle's shanty. She worked as a maid in a rich area, with her eldest daughter Suraiya, who was seventeen. She cleaned, washed clothes and cut vegetables. Her other two children, Sanjeeda, who is fourteen, and eleven-year-old Amir, mostly stay with their grandmother in a slum in Kolkata.

One day after dinner, Sana and I were just going to play outside when Aba called us back.

'Wait a minute. I want to talk to you.'

'What's happened?'

'You know Munni, don't you?'

Of course we knew Munni. She often came to see my father, and we'd seen them together in the slum a few times. Aba had introduced her to us as his friend.

'Yes, why?'

'I'm planning to marry her.'

He told us Munni had proposed and that he thought the match would be good for us. Sana and I looked at each other. We didn't mind. In fact, we were quite happy. Our parents had got divorced many years before and I didn't even remember my biological mother. I'd be happy to have a mother to look after us and the house. Besides, Munni seemed nice.

'OK, Aba!'

The wedding took place a few months later. There was a tent pitched right at the end of the main road of our slum. From early in the morning, the whole household was busy preparing food and the scent of chicken biryani floated everywhere. Our neighbours joined us in the celebration. Munni's younger children, Sanjeeda and Amir, couldn't come all the way from Kolkata, though. The journey was too long and cost too much. But Sana, Abbas and I met our new sister Suraiya. She'd been working since she was very young, helping her mother, like many of the children in the slums do. We asked her lots of questions about the house where she worked and the people she worked for. I wanted to know how rich people lived. Life outside the slums has always fascinated me and Abbas.

Two months later we moved in to Munni's house. Inside it was painted pink and very clean. It was one room, much smaller than Dadi's, in a lane on the edge of the slum with a sewer just in front and a rubbish dump right behind, stretching away as far as the eye could see. There was no tap in this part of the slum. Sanjeeda and Amir left Kolkata and came to Mumbai to move in with us. So there were six of us sleeping in a room. Me, my father, Sanjeeda, Munni and Amir sleep in a row, with Abbas in a little space at our feet. Suraiya sleeps at her employers' house. My sister Sana stayed at my grandmother's. No one else could fit into that room! But our life didn't really change. My brothers were assigned the job of getting water. They had to get up at 5 a.m. to queue up and bring back enough buckets to last a day. We got on very well with Munni straight away. She looked after us as if we were her own children. The only thing Munni doesn't like is loud noise, so I started going to my uncle's house to watch television.

I'd been asking my father for a long time to take us to Juhu Beach. Finally, he gave in, and four of us – me, my new *ami* (mother), Aba and Abbas – took a bus. It dropped us on the big, busy street that I'd dreamed about going to for ever. I ran straight for the water, surrounded by couples holding hands, families sitting together and carts full of *kacha aam*, coconuts and spicy peanuts. There were vendors selling sticks with coloured lights coming out of them, and loads of stalls selling food. *Pav bhaji is* a speciality of my city, and most of the beach stalls were selling it. It's a spicy mix of mashed vegetables served with buttered naan, onion and lemon on the side. But the only thing I wanted to eat was gola: crushed ice with coloured syrup. My favourite syrup is *kala khatta* (blackberry). After this I made my way straight to the water, though I could hear my father running behind me and shouting: 'Rubina, it's dangerous!'

I pretended I couldn't hear and ran straight to the sea, taking off my *chappals* in one hand and licking my gola from the other. The water was cool, and the sand squeezing between my toes felt lovely. It was perfect.

'Watch out, Rubina, there are waves!'

I wanted to enjoy every moment I had. I wanted to go further but my father got really angry.

'You're too far out, Rubina! Come back or we're going home now!'

I came back unwillingly; my trouser bottoms wet and full of sand. I wanted to play with the waves and sit on the wet sand for hours and hours.

A few days later I went back to Juhu Beach with

Suraiya. Being the eldest, she was quite independent. I hoped it would be more fun with her. Sanjeeda also came with us. Before we left, Ami told us to be careful and not to speak to strangers. As soon as we got off the bus, Suraiya bought me some slices of salty green mango to eat and we walked along the water's edge. Juhu Beach is always crowded and always full of vendors. It took us a little while to notice that a man was following us, but after a while he started to smile and make faces. Suraiya was older than me, but she had no idea what to do. She got scared and started walking faster. We were holding on to each other. As soon as we reached the main road, we jumped on the first bus we saw. I don't know what that man wanted, but it wasn't something good. When we got back home we didn't dare say anything to Munni. I didn't want to tell my father either. I was scared they would never let us go out alone again.

It was Suraiya who gave me my first doll. She'd brought it from Kolkata, where she'd been with Munni to visit her grandmother. Hardly anyone in the slums has got a doll. It was a fair-skinned Barbie with long golden hair. She was so pretty and I took her everywhere with me. I think all my friends were immensely jealous. I got my grandmother to make her clothes from scraps of cloth I found lying around the slums. One day, one of my friends came to see me.

'Can I sleep at your place? My mother's gone to work and there's no one at home.'

'OK, but you've got to be quiet, my mother's asleep.'

I lay on the ground next to Ami, not thinking any more about my friend, who was sleeping next to me. When I woke up, my Barbie was gone. I was shouting and crying. I was so upset to lose my only doll. One day I saw my friend playing with a doll. It looked quite different from mine and it took me a while to recognize her. She had put some dirty make-up on her face and transformed my Barbie into a *bhotni* (a ghost). She'd even put different clothes on her, ones that had never seen before. I was furious.

'What have you done to my doll?'

'It's not yours, it's mine. You can see it's different.'

'Are you kidding me? That's my doll! You've just put some make-up and some other clothes on her.'

'No, I haven't. You are going mad.'

I couldn't believe what I was hearing. I started shouting and Munni came running. My friend ran away and I kept screaming, 'That liar took my doll away!'

I had many fights with this girl, trying to get my

Barbie back, but it was no good. That *chorni* (thief) never gave it back and after a while I never spoke to her again. That was my first ever doll. I got another doll, but I didn't get to keep her long either. One of my friends found her in the dump and gave her to me as a present. The doll was in a terrible state and half her hair was missing, but I didn't care. I thought she was beautiful. One day a neighbour came to our house crying. She was shouting and beating her chest. She told my mother that her twenty-year-old daughter was possessed.

'I don't know what to do, Munni. You've got to help me.'

There are many ghosts in our neighbourhood. Ghosts are very attracted to dirty places. That's why the rubbish dump just behind our house is full of them. My new mother is very religious and knows the Koran very well. She can drive out ghosts through reading the Koran. Munni went with the lady to examine her daughter and I followed, a bit scared but curious. At the lady's house a girl was throwing herself on the dirt floor, shaking her head around. She really did look mad. I've never seen anything like her eyes, which were completely white. She was crying, but there were no tears. I was terrified. I pulled at Munni's *dupatta* (scarf).

'*Ami*, what happened to the girl?'

'She's been taken over by bad spirits. If we don't exorcize them, they'll drive her insane.'

I got out of there as fast as I could. I no longer wanted to see what Ami could do. Ghost stories scare me to death. When I got home, my doll was waiting for me in a corner. I started to play with her, but when I looked at her face I had the feeling she was looking at me in a funny way. Her eyes were like the girl's. I was horrified and threw her across the room.

I have heard many stories about spirits getting into dolls. My neighbour told me dolls get possessed easily because people get attached to them. And this doll was found in the rubbish dump, too, which is the home of many bad spirits. I grabbed the doll and threw her on to the rubbish heap behind the house. I decided from then on never to play with a doll again. I'd much rather go and play cricket or kancha. At least no ghost could enter my body that way. I was so scared that after that whenever I wanted to go to the toilet I had to take someone with me. At night, they switch off all the lights in the toilet area and I have heard many strange noises there.

5

Bollywood

'Rubiiiina! Come here!'

'What is it, Aba?'

'Come here now! Maxima is on the telephone. I think she's got something urgent to tell you!'

I was busy playing on the mud mound outside our house. I hadn't heard from Maxima for ages. She was Danny's assistant so it had to be important. I slid down the little slope and hopped on to the bricks in the murky water. I grabbed the mobile phone my father was holding out to me. He'd bought the phone not long ago so the film team could contact him. I really like mobile phones and the games they have. I know all the settings, like how to take a picture or make a video. I keep taking my own pictures all day. It's like a toy. I got the highest points on the car-racing game as well – no one can beat me at that.

I was very excited that Maxima was calling me.

'Hello?'

'Hello, Rubina, how are you?'

'Fine, thanks.'

'Rubina, the film is coming out in India in a few days and they've organized a screening for the team. You'll be able to see the film at last. Would you like that?'

'Oh yes!'

'And that's not all. On the 22nd it's the film's premiere. You and all your family are invited. Do you know what that means?'

'No.'

'It means we're going shopping! It's going to be a very glamorous evening with lots of famous actors and media. I mean, news channels. Danny wants us to buy you a beautiful dress!'

My heart was racing! I couldn't have been happier: a beautiful dress, a chance to see my movie and to see famous people. It was all too much. I told my aba: 'My movie's going to be shown in India!'

The very next day Rakesh, one of the production team, came to pick up me and Azhar and take us shopping. It was not the first time Danny had sent us shopping, but I hadn't known I'd get another opportunity. The last time I had bought two dresses, but this time shopping would be even better because I'd be getting clothes for a special occasion: my first premiere! I had to buy two dresses, one for the movie screening and the other for the function.

I was going to get a real film star's dress! Rakesh took us to a huge shop with many floors and air-conditioning. They had racks and racks of clothes. They had so many beautiful dresses, some with many layers, as well as skirts and trousers. They all were really expensive. The only market I ever go to is the one next to our slum, but they have nothing like this. Sometimes my cousin Rukhsar goes to Bandra to buy an expensive dress but that's rare. And this shop was different. I walked along the rows of hangers and touched all the fabrics. I wanted to try everything on. Azhar was messing around as usual, posing like a romantic hero in different coloured jackets. In the end, after great difficulty, I chose a long green dress with glittering gold embroidery and a matching long chiffon *dupatta* to go round my neck. It fit me like it was made for me, an outfit for a princess! Azhar also bought an Indian suit.

All of a sudden there was so much going on in my life. Two days before the premiere, we were picked up again and taken to the production studios to see the film with the rest of the cast and crew. I was going to see myself on the big screen! All the actors were there, along with the members of the production team we'd spent a whole month with: Rakesh, Loveleen *didi*, Maxima *didi* and, of course, Danny uncle, who hugged me as soon as he saw me. I had lost all hope of ever seeing Danny again. He seemed overjoyed to see us; I was certainly overjoyed to see him. I really like him. Azhar and I couldn't keep still – at last we were going to see ourselves on the big screen. When the lights were switched off and there was complete silence, I didn't know what to expect. Then there I was, running along the train, shouting and putting chillies on Azhar's willy. My eyes were glued to the screen but I was also looking at people's faces for their reactions. It was great to see myself on the screen, talking, dancing and fighting. Finally, when my song came at the end I was bursting with happiness. I was so happy I didn't know what to do with myself.

All the dialogues were translated into English, but I could understand what was going on by watching the pictures. Jamal Malik goes on the TV gameshow *Kaun Banega Crorepati?* (*Who Wants to be a Millionaire?*) so that he can find Latika, the girl he loves. Jamal is a slumdog, but even though he's never been to school, he knows plenty about life.

Because of all his experience and knowledge, he's able to answer all the questions and win the prize. The best thing about the movie is that it shows that a slum child can also become rich through his hard work. Of course, it's just a film, but it gives hope. I was amazed by how realistic everything looked. When I hunched my shoulders under the rain, it really looked like real rain, not machine rain, and the *mirchi* scene was also superb. The lights went up and it took me a while to come back to reality. It was like my own life, but better! I was so happy to be part of it I couldn't speak. Around me all the cast and crew were congratulating each other warmly. My father was so proud of me, I could see it in his eyes. Everyone was patting us on our shoulders or taking us in their arms, saying, '*Bahut accha*, Rubina. Really good.'

They all kept repeating strange words, too: 'Gulden glubs' and 'Oskers'. In the end Loveleen told me what it was they were all so excited about.

'*Slumdog Millionaire* won four prizes at the Golden Globes ten days ago. It's fantastic news!'

'*Gulden Glubs* – what are they?'

'It's a big ceremony in the United States, giving prizes to the year's best films.'

'United States, *kya hai*?'

'The United States is America – Hollywood!'

America? I'd heard of it, but it didn't mean much to me. Apart from Kolkata, all I knew was Mumbai. I thought it was the capital of India, but I wasn't sure. One thing was sure: I didn't know much about other countries except India. All I knew about 'America' was that it was very far away. But these 'Gulden Glubs' had to be very important from the way everyone in the room was so happy.

Loveleen went on excitedly, 'I can't wait for the Oscar nominations!'

I didn't really understand what it all meant, but I joined in the celebrations as I was truly happy to see myself on the screen. I couldn't wait to tell my family all about it. On the way back home Azhar and I just couldn't stop talking.

'Did you see the scene where I fell off the train roof?'

'Did you see me dancing "Ringa Ringa"?'

'Did you see Ayush falling in to the poo?'

When we came back home, I couldn't stop talking about the movie to my cousins, uncle, aunt, Abbas, Sana and Amir. I told them they could see my movie in the cinema. They were showing trailers for it, and every time it came on people started to cheer me and shout out my name, 'Rubina, Rubina!' Before the premiere, a few reporters from the news channel came to meet me. They were asking me questions and getting me to pose for pictures. Everything was going too fast for me.

That Thursday morning some foreign reporters came. After an interview, they asked me and Azhar to dance on the railway track alongside our slum. I was surprised that even foreign reporters knew about me. By the afternoon everybody was rushing about. My family was asking me to take some rest and not to get dirty. My father, Munni, grandmother and also Abbas were coming with me for the premiere. Munni wanted to look good and had bought herself a lovely pink sari. When I put on my green dress, my sister Sana was speechless at first, and then she came over to touch the chiffon and look at the fine work on the front. To make the whole outfit perfect she insisted on lending me her jewellery. I put kohl in my eyes and thick eyeliner on top and at the end I applied some pink lipstick. At last we were ready. On my way out of the slum, everyone was looking at me admiringly.

'Kya lag rahi. Rubina, you're looking great.'

Parvesh was given the responsibility of taking me and Azhar to the premiere at the IMAX, one of Mumbai's biggest cinemas. We were supposed to leave exactly at six in the evening. When I came out, Azhar was already waiting. He wore a long maroon *kurta* with white *dupatta*. He looked so different in this outfit. He was also going to the premiere with his mother and father. Parvesh wanted to take us all in a bus but Azhar's father refused to get on. He started shouting that Parvesh is cheating us by taking the transport money from the crew and then taking us all in a bus. I didn't want to go in a crowded bus either. I was scared of spoiling my dress and make-up. After many fights, we took taxis to Wadala, a suburb of Mumbai. We had to take two taxis as we couldn't fit in one. Azhar, his family and Parvesh went in one and me and my family in another. It took us more than an hour and a half to reach Wadala. To make matters worse, our taxi broke down on the way. I nearly cried. I didn't want to be late for the most important day of my life.

We got there at around 8.30. There was a huge crowd outside blocking the way in. Dozens of photographers and cameramen were pointing their cameras at us. The production crew was waiting for us at the other gate and I went inside with them. My family was supposed to come from the other side. Outside there was total chaos with so many reporters with huge cameras and mikes. When I went inside everyone was already there – I was the last one to arrive. They told me the whole team would walk the red carpet together. I saw Loveleen looking nice in a pink sari, Tanay all handsome in his black velvet suit with a purple scarf. Danny came over to welcome us and hugged Azhar and me. Everyone was also eagerly waiting for the Oscar nominations. I'd heard people saying that this is the highest praise for the best films. Finally the magical moment arrived. There were musicians with *dhol* drums walking in front of us along the red carpet and the whole crew followed behind. Everyone was dancing: Loveleen *didi*, Anil Kapoor, Dev Patel and even Danny uncle danced with us. The reporters were shouting my name 'Rubina, Rubina', and I knew I had become a star. Loveleen told me later that our movie had been chosen for the Oscars in ten different categories. It didn't matter to me that much. For me, this was my night.

My eyes were popping out! There were Hrithik Roshan, Imran Khan, Kareena Kapoor, Amrita Rao, Aamir Khan, Deepika Padukone and loads of other actors. It seemed that all the actors and actresses of Bollywood had turned out to the IMAX to see my film. Even my idol Preity Zinta was there. She wore a beautiful long white dress. Some actors were in long dresses or black suits. Others were in short dresses for the women, jeans and T-shirts for the men. They were all having a good time, chatting and having a drink. Munni was intimidated at first, seeing all those famous actors, but she was super-excited, unable to decide where to point her camera next.

I felt like a real film star. Once inside the cinema, my parents sat down next to Azhar's. Azhar and I kept looking all around to see who was behind us. At last, the film started. Munni and Aba had all their attention on the screen and didn't say a word. Azhar and I kept laughing every time we saw ourselves! The lights came up after the movie was over and there was a long, loud burst of clapping. I thought the cheering would never stop. When we went out, loads of people came to hug and congratulate me, including big stars like Kareena Kapoor and Hrithik Roshan.

'Bravo, Rubina, you were brilliant! Keep on doing what you're doing!'

'*Shukria.*'

Hrithik Roshan came to speak to me? Munni was amazed. I asked for his autograph – you don't meet a superstar like him every day. Meanwhile, Danny kept saying good things about me to my father:

'So you're Rubina's father? You're a lucky man! She's got a real gift, your daughter. On set she acted as though she'd been doing it all her life.'

'Thank you, sir.'

My father doesn't speak English, so he didn't understand everything, but he did understand that nice things were being said about his daughter and he couldn't stop smiling. Anil Kapoor came over to say a few words to my father and me.

'Rubina is a lovely kid and a really talented actress. Take care of her, make sure she gets an education and she'll go far, you'll see!'

I think my father realized that day how this film has changed my life. The next day the film went on general release and he rushed to the Gaiety Galaxy cinema near the slum to see it in Hindi this time. When he came back he was more thrilled then ever as he'd been able to understand all the dialogue. He really liked the story, with the slum as the background. It was like seeing our everyday life on the big screen. The Dharavi slums where the film was shot are not so different from the Bandra East slums. He was especially excited to see the reactions of people sitting next to him. He was proud to be my aba.

The whole of Mumbai was showing our movie poster. Every turn, there was a poster. Some were in Hindi, others in English. I was in seventh heaven and couldn't stop thanking Allah for it.

This film is a bit different from other Bollywood movies in that it shows real things. Like the issue of Hindus and Muslims fighting, and when the two heroes, Jamal and Salim, see their own mother die before their very eyes. In reality these fights did happen in the Mumbai slums. It was before I was born, but my father remembers it as if it happened yesterday. He told me about it. He was a teenager at the time when the Hindus and the Muslims had a big clash in our slum. My father ran to hide like everyone else. Some people had knives, others guns. Aba saw a man fall dead next to him, hit by a *goli* (bullet). Three of his neighbours were also killed. The police came, but they just added to the panic, killing more people. There were lots of children among the victims. Since then everything has gone back to normal. The Hindus and Muslims live side by side without too many problems but there is still some tension. I sometimes wonder why they hate each other. We are all the same people from the same country, but I guess it is because there are some bad people in both communities. I have a few Hindu friends and I also celebrate Diwali, the festival of lights and crackers. You have to be careful of crackers in the slums, though, or you could cause a huge fire. We set them off just outside, near the railway tracks.

As for the trafficking of handicapped children that you see in *Slumdog Millionaire*, that's all true too. In the film, the three heroes, Jamal, Salim and Latika, are picked up by child-sellers who keep them in a kind of orphanage. They blind them or cut off one of their legs before sending them out to beg. I'd already heard about this, but I'd never seen it happen to any of the children in our slum. My father told me it didn't happen to children with parents. The ones in danger were orphans who were forced to live on the streets. Aba had never seen a film like this, so different from the other movies.

My father wasn't the only one to think it was an interesting film. After the premiere and the release of the movie, many journalists became interested in our slum and in me. The day after the premiere, special cars with round discs attached to the roofs started coming. They wanted to interview me about the making of the film and my experiences, but they were more interested in the conditions I lived in. It was strange to see them getting so excited about a few shacks and some rubbish and the sewage drains. Our neighbours were surprised at first to see all these new people, but even they got used to it. Whenever a team of reporters were on their way, kids would run and tell me, 'Rubina! There is a camera coming for you.'

After I'd finished shooting the film, our neighbours didn't ask me about it. But after *Slumdog Millionaire* was released in India, everything changed. Now it wasn't just my cousins and brother but all the slum kids dancing to 'Ringa Ringa' and 'Jai Ho'.

Azhar and I found ourselves in the spotlight. All of a sudden it seemed the whole world was interested in me. My friends all came to see me in turn, full of all kinds of questions about making the film, the stars I'd met or the special effects. Our house was always full of people. The kids at school, who'd now seen us on the red carpet on TV, were fascinated. Even Parvesh became very important. Every day parents met him to ask him to take their kids for auditions, too.

6

The best day of my life

'Can you believe it, Rubina? You're going to America! America, Rubina!'

Loveleen called my father after the premiere to tell him that the whole team of *Slumdog Millionaire* would be going to the Oscars awards. Aba was a bit scared at the thought of me travelling so far. But I was going mad thinking about America. I thought it would be full of fair-coloured people with golden hair. I kept wondering whether they had slums like ours in America. I was full of questions and excited at the same time. It took my father a few days to make up his mind. In the end, he discussed it with many relatives and friends, who all agreed that he couldn't say no to an opportunity like this. Once he'd decided, Aba, who was usually so calm, couldn't keep still. He was even more excited than me . . . I told myself that America had to be a lot of fun if everyone was making so much fuss about it. For me, it was another step and more things to discover.

'Father, how far is America?'

'Rubina, America is probably seven oceans away.'

'So do we get there by boat?'

'No, in a plane.'

'I'm going to go in a plane?'

'Yes, Rubina, you're going to fly in the sky.'

I'd seen aeroplanes flying over our slum. I'd also been to a plane park in Juhu where they have this big plane made from bricks. It doesn't move but I used to love going inside and pretending that it might fly in the sky at any moment. I always wondered how things would look from the sky. Everything would be so tiny. But I'd never imagined that one day I'd get a chance to be inside a real flying plane. I was actually going to be flying higher than the clouds! The only thing worrying me was travelling so far on my own.

'Aba, you will come with me, won't you?'

'I'm afraid I can't, because of my ankle. It's still not completely fine. I don't want to have problems in a country that's such a long way away.'

'Do I have to go on my own then?'

'Don't worry; I know who will go with you. Come with me.'

Aba left the house, and I followed him, skipping my way through the rubbish. At the end of the narrow street, we quickly turned right to my uncle's house. My father pushed aside the curtain to enter the house and greeted his brother. I was just behind him and I went in as well. My uncle was lying on the bed and I could smell that my aunt was making yummy mutton curry. Aba began speaking with a little smile.

'Guess what, Mohiuddin?'

'What?'

'You're going to America with Rubina.'

'*Kya?*'

'I will come and see you tomorrow morning because we need to discuss it. *Khuda hafiz!*'

My uncle was shocked. He thought my aba was joking. I giggled and left as well, as if I had no idea what all this was about. For the next few days I just kept dreaming about America. All the slum kids had their own ideas about the place.

'It's so far away, Rubina.'

'It's full of fat people, Rubina.'

'It's full of really rich people. They have enormous cars, and fair hair.'

My friends were laughing and smacking me on the back.

One day Rakesh and Adnan from the film production company turned up at our house. I was happy to see them because it meant news about my America trip.

'Hello, Rafiq, we're here to collect the documents for the passport application. Has your brother got everything ready?'

'I don't know, let's go and see.'

At my uncle's house, Aba introduced the two men.

'Mohiuddin, this is Rakesh and Adnan. They need identity papers for your passport application.'

'Passport?'

'Yes, a passport. You know, I told you about going to America!'

My uncle just stood there with his mouth wide open. Rakesh looked worried and said that we needed to hurry.

'Mohiuddin, we've got to move fast. The Oscar ceremony is on 22 February and it takes a long time to get a passport. And on top of that we have to apply for a visa to go America, and we have to buy the plane tickets.'

I understood 'passport' but wondered what 'visa' was all about. Rakesh told me that a visa was a stamp on the passport that said you could go to America.

Azhar's parents also took a long time to decide that

108

Azhar would be going to the United States with his mother. In the end, everything was done in a hurry and it was a mad panic, and Danny really thought that Azhar and I wouldn't get there in time. Even I was scared I might not get the passport and a visa. I was very excited about this trip. The film production company stepped in to speed up the process. It was quite difficult. I didn't have all the documents. No one in my family knew my exact date of birth and I didn't even have a birth certificate. The production company decided I was born on 21 January 1999. I went with my uncle and Azhar to the passport office. Finally, I had my passport. But I had to get my visa too, and it was already 20 February. I was so scared – what if they didn't give me a visa? But finally I got my visa and now I knew nothing could stop me from going to 'AMERICA'. I was over the moon.

The next day was crazy. I had to pack and there were journalists chasing us. Click, click went their cameras. I tried to tell them to go away. We were in a hurry, we didn't need distractions. Soon it was the day of our departure. Even before we left for the airport, some journalists turned up to interview us in Bandra East slum.

'So, Rubina, are you pleased you're going?'

'Very happy! I can't wait!'

'What does America mean to you?'

'I don't know, but I'll take loads of photos to show my friends and family when I get back.'

'Have you bought a pretty dress for the ceremony?'

'No, we'll buy my dress in America.'

'What about you, Mohiuddin, what will you be wearing?'

'I think jeans and a nice T-shirt.'

At last the taxi came to take us to the international airport. Airports are so different from railway stations, so clean and shiny. There was no big crowd and people were not pushing or shoving. We had to get our bags checked, and they also checked me with a long rod machine, which makes a beeping sound. Inside the plane, I wasn't scared. I was busy exploring. There was a small television screen in front of our seats and a button above us. If you press that button, a *didi* comes and you can ask her for candies, cold drinks or anything else. When the plane started to move slowly along the road, I felt a great joy. With my face pressed up against the window, I saw the landscape pass by and then, suddenly, my heart skipped a beat: we left the ground with a loud noise.

I couldn't help crying out. My uncle Mohiuddin smiled a little and was trying to reassure me, but I could see he was a bit tense and scared too. This was also his first time. Azhar and I couldn't sit still. We tried all the buttons, all the seat positions, all the channels on the TV screen. They even had a cartoon channel. I loved it when they brought us a meal on a tray and some sweets as well. Flying was great fun. Some people came to me during the flight to ask for my autograph. I couldn't believe it! I gave them my autograph, carefully writing my name in English and revelling in my own glory. After several hours, I drowsily felt the aircraft going down.

'What's happening?'

'The plane is going to land.'

When we landed, I didn't know what to expect. At the exit, we walked along some long, brightly lit corridors.

'Is this America?'

'No, this is Germany. We're going to catch another plane.'

I had never heard about Germany before. I realized how far America is. This airport was very different from the one in Mumbai: everything was so cool and smelled so fresh. It looked brand new. We took another plane an hour later. This time, when the plane took off, I wasn't surprised. I knew what to expect. It was a very long journey and I was getting tired, though I slept a bit also. The pilot finally announced that we were landing in Los Angeles. Los

Angeles . . . I didn't know anything about that city. I'd never even heard the name before.

Loveleen explained: 'The city of Los Angeles is where Hollywood is.'

'What's Hollywood?'

'Bollywood is in Mumbai and Hollywood is in America.'

'Do the Americans make a lot of films?'

'Yes, loads!'

Los Angeles airport was even bigger and more beautiful than the one in Germany. The corridors and waiting rooms were vast. We went through an endless series of checks and controls. At the exit, we were met by a man from the production company. It was nearly twenty-four hours since I had left Mumbai and everyone felt a little lost and tired. There was a black car waiting for us outside, and my tiredness suddenly vanished. I had never seen such a nice car in my life. Inside, it was spacious and there was even a little fridge filled with Coca-Cola! On the road, we passed loads of beautiful houses that looked huge and had big gardens filled with flowers.

In America the roads are not littered with rubbish. Everything was clean, spotless. The strangest thing was that I didn't see anyone walking: everyone seemed to have a car here. It looked empty compared to Mumbai. After driving for half an hour, we arrived at the hotel. It was even more beautiful than the one where I'd met Danny uncle in Mumbai. When we went inside, it took my breath away. None of us could stop admiring it. The first thing I saw were two swimming pools, one of which was huge. Before my uncle and Azhar's mother could react, Azhar and I had run towards the smaller one, taken off our clothes and jumped in. The water was quite warm, which was good because it was cold here compared to Mumbai. I particularly liked the bubbles that rose up from the bottom and tickled our bodies. It was so much fun.

Azhar's mum rushed over shouting: 'Azhar, will you get out of the water? You'll catch a cold!'

My uncle just looked at me without saying a word: he knew very well there was no point. Azhar and I continued to jump around in the bubbles without paying any attention to the hotel guests, who were watching us as though we were animals from a jungle. After a few minutes, though, we had to get out of the pool.

'Children, you must get out of the water now. Azhar's mum is right, you'll catch a cold. And if you're ill, you won't be able to go to the party tonight.'

'A party? What party?'

'A party organized for the film team in a hotel. You need to get ready.'

I was excited about going to a party. We wrapped ourselves in the white towels that were held out to us. We took a lift from the main area to go to our rooms on the fourth floor of this luxury hotel, which I thought was lovely. This was the first time I'd stayed somewhere other than in the slum. Azhar's room, which he was sharing with his mother, was just opposite ours. It was a huge room, so vast I could have cycled around in it, and the bathroom was as big as our home in the slum. There was also a small fridge.

The person escorting us explained: 'In this fridge there are chocolates, drinks, biscuits and crisps. If you're hungry, help yourselves. And if you need anything at all, don't hesitate to ask. Just dial number nine for the reception.'

While Mohiuddin opened the suitcases to unpack, I ran around the room to discover all its wonders: in the bathroom was a big tub (the first I'd ever seen in my life!), with all kinds of amazing-smelling things: bottles of shampoo, tubes of cream, soap, sweets, towels, and loads of other things I couldn't wait to try. From the windows, I could see some wonderful white and pink flowers. The room had two big beds separated by a small table with a lamp

114

on it. The beds were so soft I could sink in them and bounce up and down. There was an enormous television screen, flat like a newspaper. I pounced on the remote to find out what channels were on offer. But just then, someone knocked on the door; it was a woman.

'Hi, I'm Tessy. I'll be looking after you during your stay.'

'Hi, I'm Rubina, and this is my uncle, Mohiuddin.'

'Nice to meet you. Have you been told that there's a party this evening? I've brought you a pretty dress to wear. Would you like to see it?'

'Yes!'

Tessy was really nice. She bought me a gorgeous pink sleeveless dress and flowery sandals for the party. Pink is not my favourite colour but I was excited because it was an American dress.

'I thought this colour would really suit you. Do you like it?'

'I love it!'

The sandals were a little small, but I managed. With my hair still damp after my dip in the bubbling pool, I slipped on my new dress and looked in the mirror. Tessy told me it was time to leave and we went down in a huge and shiny lift to the lobby of the hotel to meet Azhar, Ayush, Tanay, Ashutosh and Tanvi, the other child actors in the film. All of us were staying at the InterContinental Hotel. We climbed back in to the car and were driven to another hotel, where the party was being held. When he saw us arrive, Danny rushed over to us.

'Welcome to America!'

He kissed each of us warmly. Then he introduced us to his wife and three children, two daughters and a son, who looked as nice as him. His family were very friendly and his son wanted to dance with me. I couldn't stop giggling. The entire team of *Slumdog Millionaire* was reunited, along with their families. Several people came up to me and asked for an autograph. It was still strange but I was getting used to it. I took a great deal of care over each one. We were served fruit juice, but I didn't touch any of the snacks I was offered. They looked really strange. After an hour, I was tired and yawning. It seemed that I had been up for ever, but it was only 7 p.m. The time difference made it feel much later to me. Danny was very understanding.

'Go back and get some sleep, kids. You've got to be on top form tomorrow.'

The driver took us back to the hotel with Azhar, who was just as exhausted as I was. At least, for once, he was too tired to fight with me. Back in our room, I looked at the large bed with its clean white sheets. I'd never slept alone: at home we were used to huddling together in a small space. There was so much room here, it was too much for me. I tried but I couldn't sleep. The mattress, the room: everything was too spacious. My uncle was sleeping in the bed next to me, but it wasn't the same. I put on my nightdress and went across the corridor to knock on the door opposite. Azhar's mum opened the door.

'Rubina? What's the matter?'

'Can I sleep in your bed with you?'

All three of us got in to the same bed. Even with three of us, we felt scared in that enormous room. Azhar and his mother weren't used to these things either, and were having a hard time. We cuddled up together and finally fell asleep, completely exhausted. The next morning, we woke up very early, feeling great. The feeling that I was in America still hadn't sunk in. We immediately raced down from the fourth floor of the hotel to plunge in to the pool. In Bandra East, I bathe every day in a drainage tank just behind the mud mound. This tank is just the size of our room and it has huge, thick pipes running over it. All the local kids gather there when it's hot. The water is totally black with litter and old *chappals* and wrappers floating on the surface, but it's the only place to cool down. I would climb down, using pieces of cloth tied around small pipes.

Some boys would jump from the top, splashing everyone around them. I wouldn't have missed these daily sessions for anything; I loved being in the water. It wasn't deep but I used to pretend to dive from the corner steps. I dived exactly the way you see it on the television with my hands pressed together. Very few boys in the slum know how to swim, but everyone knows how to splash about. In this tank you just had to be careful not to swallow the water. Once some water went in my mouth and it was really bitter. There are also snakes on the bottom, which can bite you if you step on them. Women come here to wash clothes too.

I never used to bathe in my house. There were always cockroaches in that little corner and water has to be used carefully as there is so little of it. I preferred to have a quick dip in the drainage tank, which was much more fun. In Los Angeles, the water was clean, totally clear, and the pool was as big as a lake. It was even better than at Juhu Beach, where you couldn't bathe properly because of the waves. I never used that bathtub in my hotel room, except once, to clean my hair. You can't put soap and shampoo on and jump in this pool, though. I found that strange.

After I learned what it was called, 'Jacuzzi', I kept repeating the strange word. We stayed in it all morning. My uncle and Azhar's mother had a great deal of trouble getting us to come out.

In this hotel there were many restaurants. But Americans eat different food to us. There was no *dal*, no *chawal* or chicken masala, but odd, strange-tasting things. It was all so tasteless. Hardly any spices in it. I could never get used to their 'pizzas', a type of chapati covered with tomato sauce and some white stuff. They also had potatoes cut into long strips but again just with salt and no curry. I was already very fussy back home. My grandmother often said, 'Stop playing with your food! Learn to eat everything!'

All the same, she always made sure she prepared my favourite meals. In America, though, there was really nothing I liked, except biscuits, bars of chocolate and noodles, which they called 'pasta' there. Again they weren't spicy but they had some taste. There were two colour pastas available: one that was white, which I didn't like much, and the other that had red sauce with some vegetable, which was OK. After lunch, we went out to explore the place. Later, Tessy came to see us at the hotel. In my room, she spread out a number of dresses on the bed for me.

'Here, choose the one you'd like to wear tonight for your big night, Rubina!'

There were at least twenty, along with the matching

shoes and hair pins. I kept going from one to another, unable to decide. I wanted to have all of them. In the end, I chose one made of silk: it was sky blue, the colour of the water in the pool. But I had difficulty with the shoes as they didn't fit. Tessy had to call and get another pair.

'Stay here; someone will come to help you get ready. I'll see you soon; I'm going to see to the others.'

A woman arrived shortly after. She helped me to put on my beautiful dress, slipped my feet in to the white shoes, then adjusted the layers of my dress, before tying the big ribbon at the back. She also spent a long time doing my hair, opting for a thin, silver-coloured hair band.

'Aren't you going to put any make-up on me?'

'Oh no, you're pretty enough like that! It's much better to look natural, honestly.'

'OK . . .'

I was a little disappointed: I loved putting kohl on my eyes. Perhaps this is not the fashion in America. She told me no kids wear make-up here. But I was hoping to have some American make-up on my face. Fortunately, I had some pretty henna motifs that Rukhsar had applied to my hands and forearms before I left. My uncle was wearing a jacket he had brought with him. Since he wasn't attending the ceremony in the main auditorium, he didn't have to look as elegant as me. I couldn't stop looking at myself in a long mirror. The woman told me to sit nicely so I didn't crush my dress before the ceremony. I thought this might be like the premiere, but then this is America and they do everything differently here.

We all met up in the hotel lobby. Tanvi, the child actress who played Latika when she was a bit older, looked very beautiful in her old rose dress. All the boys were wearing black suits with a white shirt and bowtie. Even that clown, Azhar, looked sophisticated. While waiting for the car to pick us up, we took loads of photos of ourselves sitting on the comfortable sofas in the lobby. We were all complimenting each other. I threw lots of different poses. Sometimes Azhar had the camera, sometimes it was me. One of the hotel employees took a photo of us all together, Azhar, Ayush, Tanvi, Tanay, Ashutosh and me: all the child actors from *Slumdog Millionaire*. The bellboy then wanted his photo taken with us. We were all excited and couldn't stop talking about our big night.

'Get in the car, children.'

This was no ordinary car. It was very long. It looked like a mini train with black windows and enough space inside to fit my whole class. I'd never ever seen anything like it in Mumbai. They told me the name of the car but it is too difficult for me to remember. My uncle and Azhar's mother climbed in to another car. On the way, we poured ourselves fruit juices and some Coca-Cola into glasses that had been placed on top of a little fridge just for us. When we arrived at the Kodak Theater, where the Oscar function was being held, there were even more people than at the premiere in Mumbai. The place was huge. The cameras were waiting for us as soon as we climbed out of the car. Even the reporters were dressed nicely. I smiled at everyone. Danny and the rest of the film team were waiting for us on the red carpet. Then I saw Preity Zinta. She was wearing a gorgeous royal blue satin dress. There were so many other beautiful women there. They all looked like Barbies. Tanay and Ashutosh, who were the oldest among us, began jumping up and down.

'Have you seen all these stars? Look at them all!'

Obviously, I figured all those women in amazing dresses and those men in dinner jackets were celebrities, but I didn't know a single one. I'd never seen a foreign film in my life. Frieda Pinto was looking lovely in a blue dress. She and Tanay occasionally whispered who was who in my ear.

'See that tall blonde woman, that's Nicole Kidman!'

'And that's Penelope Cruz.'

Azhar didn't know who all those people were either, but as soon as he saw a star being chased by the photographers, he went over to ask for their autograph. Then I met one actress called Angelina Jolie, who congratulated me on my role in *Slumdog Millionaire*. I started blushing. Then I asked for her autograph and . . . she asked for mine in return! When I saw A. R. Rahman, the composer of the music for *Slumdog*, I rushed over to him.

'I wanted to tell you that I love your music!'

'Thank you, I'm very touched! You did a very good job too, you know.'

The journalists also paid me loads of compliments. They lined up to ask us questions. Finally, everyone went in to the auditorium. My uncle and Azhar's mother watched the awards show on a big screen in another room. In the main auditorium, we all sat together, hanging on to every word said by the host of the ceremony. As the names of the winners were read out for each category, we became more and more excited. *Slumdog Millionaire* had already won many awards. I particularly liked the part of the ceremony where A. R. Rahman came on the stage to sing 'Jai Ho'. I was also singing and swaying to the tune. And it wasn't just me, it seemed everyone was enjoying the song. I was very happy that he got not one but two awards. I felt that my song must be really famous to have got such a big award. But I knew that the most important one would be the last one.

'And now, the Oscar for the best film.'

Everyone was silent and the whole team was praying and hoping that it would be *Slumdog Millionaire*. The ceremony had started four hours ago. The waiting was unbearable. We had to listen again to the list of nominees, then the little envelope was at last torn open.

'And the winner is . . .'

Azhar and I held our breath.

'. . . *Slumdog Millionaire*!'

We all screamed at the same time. Everyone started to hug each other and then Danny stood up to go on stage and the entire film team followed him. The crowd was cheering us and the clapping didn't stop. Because I was at the back of the stage, Dev Patel lifted me up and put me on his shoulders so I wouldn't miss anything. And then the Oscar was passed round and I found myself waving the famous award in the air. We didn't just win one Oscar, we walked off with eight! In my slum, all the kids dream of becoming actors. If a slumgirl could win an Oscar, there was no reason why a slumdog couldn't win millions, was there?

The rest of the evening passed so fast I couldn't comprehend it. After the ceremony, we were all invited to the Governor's Ball, which they told me is a very big party. I even had a little champagne. It was the first time I'd drunk alcohol and it didn't even make me dizzy. Danny uncle opened the bottle and some of it spilled. Then he offered a little to everyone. They told me to have some as we were celebrating our success. At dinner, I sat between Azhar and Dev Patel, who teased me when he caught me looking at my plate in annoyance.

'You don't like pizza then?'

'Not really . . .'

'Great, I'll have a piece then!'

I wasn't very hungry anyway. I was more tired than anything else, what with the awards ceremony, leaving the theatre with cameras clicking from all sides, then the interviews with journalists, the congratulations from everyone and the journey to the Governor's residence. And it had only just begun: after dinner, we went to a party at a hotel, then we were taken to another party and then another . . . Each time, we danced for five minutes and then we left. In the end, I'd had enough. Azhar and Ayush were in the same state as me. There were journalists everywhere wanting to talk to us. Azhar, after a time, got fed up and was getting angry.

'No more questions, I just want to sleep! Leave me alone!'

I didn't lose my cool, but I answered half asleep, feeling my eyelids growing very heavy. After five parties and countless interviews, we went back to the hotel. In my room, I took off my beautiful clothes and then slipped off to Azhar's room, where I cuddled up against him and his mother. In no time at all, I was fast asleep.

7

'Hey, kids, would you like to go and see Mickey Mouse?'

The next morning, we woke up late. The excitement of the Oscars and the parties we went to was too much. I was still finding it hard to believe it was all happening to me. I thanked Allah for letting me see a day like this. Tessy came in to the room asking us to hurry up as we were all going to a theme park called Disneyland. It was our fun day. I hadn't been to parks with rides except the one behind Baba Hospital where Aba sometimes took us. It had a swing and a few slides. So I didn't know what exactly to expect here. But I was looking forward to a day of *masti* (fun).

I know very little about Hollywood stars, but

127

because I watched cartoons on television I knew about the Disney characters. I was more thrilled about seeing Mickey Mouse and Donald Duck than I was about the stars last night. All the children got ready, and even my uncle and Azhar's mother came with us. Tessy and the bodyguards, who'd been following us around since we arrived in Los Angeles, were also there. I didn't understand why we needed bodyguards. Who wanted to harm us here?

We got to Disneyland around lunchtime. I'd never set foot in this type of park before. I knew it would be big but I never guessed how big. It must have been twice as large as my slum, or even bigger. This place was awesome. There were no poor people here.

They told us we could try as many different rides as we wanted. There were dozens of attractions and I was determined to try everything. Mickey Mouse and other cartoon characters were walking around. They were so cute – I shook hands with them. Then I did this funny dance with Mickey Mouse and Donald Duck. I didn't know where to start and which rides to try first. All these rides use *bijli*. They're not like swings where someone has to push you.

I also had the biggest thrill of my life! I loved what they called the roller coaster, which is a ride in a car on tracks. They put a belt around you to make sure you don't fall. It starts slowly, then it reaches the top, then with this huge sound it starts to go down and you feel as if you're going to crash. It was amazing. Everyone started to scream, especially when you got to the top of the slope and then it suddenly began to go down at incredible speed. I didn't know it was going to be like that. I thought it would be like a slow train ride, but this was really fast. My uncle, who was sitting next to me, was white with fear. When we got off the ride I thought he'd throw up, he was so dizzy. When I suggested we go on it again, he refused! After that, he wouldn't even go on a boat ride.

Azhar's mother refused to go on any rides. As for Azhar, he kept up his habit of calling me stupid names, though he was quiet for a while after the roller coaster. Of course, we had some good laughs together, but mostly he was irritating. He loved driving people crazy, even his mother.

'Amma, pretend to be a ghost, please.'

'That's enough, Azhar, calm down.'

'Amma, Amma, Amma, Amma, pretend to be a ghost!'

Sometimes, his mother gave in to her son's nagging. But this one even I loved. She could turn her eyelids over and then show us the whites of her eyes, and she really looked like a ghost. Azhar would run around yelling, 'Ouououuhhhh'. We laughed like crazy. On the other hand, when he called me 'rotten roti', I didn't think twice about spitting on him.

Once, when journalists were interviewing us individually, I heard him reply: 'Rubina? Oh, no, I don't like her at all, haven't you noticed how ugly she is?'

When asked about my relationship with Azhar, I gave a similar reply: 'Azhar? That pumpkin? I can't stand him!'

Obviously, we made sure that we said horrible things about each other at the tops of our voices so that the other didn't miss a single word. But once, when he thought I was looking the other way, I heard him reply: 'Rubina? Yes, she's very pretty. And she's really nice too.'

I'd return the compliment on camera. But that was it. On the roller coaster, though, I didn't hear a single 'monkey' or 'chapati-face'. He was too scared to open his mouth! As for me, I wanted to go on that ride again and again. I would even have liked the roller coaster to go faster. I also really liked the Tower of Horror: everything was dark inside and it was terrifying, particularly when the ghost chased us with his sword! I kept going back to that Tower of Horror again and again, even though my uncle wasn't keen on it at all and couldn't understand how I could enjoy being scared to death. Madhur (the actor who plays the grown-up Salim) and I tried out a two-seater eggshell kind of ride. In this we also had to wear a jacket that doubled as a safety belt. The shell then moved around in all directions and we were rocked from side to side and even turned upside down. This ride was like a mixer in which you make juice. I was completely shaken and my hair was on my face. I wondered how they made such rides. In case of emergency, you could press a button and the shell would immediately stop moving. Madhur and I never pressed the button, although we screamed so much.

Then they gave us a burger to eat, which looked like a *vada pav*, an Indian-style burger – a bun with some potato and spices in it. It's served with a sprinkling of tamarind or coriander sauce. But this was a much less tasty version with only long potato and salt to eat with it.

When we got back to the hotel, it was 11 p.m. The next morning, Danny uncle took the whole film team to the beach. There were loads of things to do there. It was much fancier than Juhu Beach. The water was dark blue and it looked much cleaner. Danny played with us and also went on the merry-go-round just like a kid. I won a soft toy bear on one of the rides, which was supposed to be very scary. Danny and I played our favourite game, where he puts his hands out and I try to slap them before he snatches them away. He asked us whether we liked this country. For me, America is the best country in the world, except for the food. At lunch, I didn't touch the chicken roll on my plate: I just didn't like the look of it. They make food very differently here, and I'm used to eating my spicy slum food. Still, that day, the last I spent in America, was perfect. Everyone was relaxed and happy. In the evening, Tessy took us shopping in town. We went to a big building with many shops and lights all around. Everything is so grand in America. There were also stairs on which you just need to stand and they take you up. I was sure that in America they had machines for everything. With a few dollars that Tessy gave me, I bought an orange T-shirt for my father. After that, I didn't want to do any more shopping. I went back to the car to rest and wait for the others. I dozed off straight away. When the the others came back to the car, I was fast asleep.

All the children had already been given a red bag. I had no idea what was inside the bag but when we opened it I couldn't stop screaming. Inside there was a camera and a laptop. I was going to be the only person in Bandra East slum to have one. I will capture many more amazing moments with my new camera. I didn't know how to use a computer but I wanted to learn.

Next day, Danny uncle came to the hotel to say goodbye. We were leaving for Mumbai, so it was the last time I saw him. I was very sad to leave Danny uncle and I didn't know when I would see him again. He spoke to me in English for a few minutes, but because Loveleen wasn't there to translate, I didn't understand much. I said, 'Thank you, Uncle Danny, for everything,' and then he left. I felt like crying.

If my father hadn't been waiting for me in India, I'd have stayed in America all my life.

8

'How was America?'

When we landed in Mumbai on 26 February, and saw that huge crowd of people and reporters who'd come to greet us like we were the biggest stars, it was then that I understood the importance of the Oscars. The screaming, the clicking of cameras, the big cars hired by the production company and the police escort through the city. But I was in no hurry to get back to my slums. In the car on the way back from the airport, my father had told me: 'And that's nothing compared to the welcome in store for you at home. Everyone's waiting for you and Azhar. You're real stars now!'

It had all been moving so fast. I needed to slow down before I could face that crowd. Seeing my worried expression, Aba went on to say: 'Don't

135

worry; we're not going back immediately. First, we're going to eat in Bandra.'

We hardly ever went out to eat lunch in a restaurant, but he wanted to make an exception because this was such a special occasion. Still, we had cars following us, but we somehow managed to escape them. We went to this nice Muslim restaurant. Everyone seemed excited but I was feeling tired and I missed America. I ordered some mutton biryani, happy to have some normal food after so long, and the aroma of that biryani made me hungrier and hungrier. I was eating big mouthfuls and my brother couldn't stop laughing.

'So you didn't get to eat anything in America!'

But I was in no mood for jokes. My father and little brother were dying to hear about my trip, but looking at my mood, they decided not to ask me any questions. I felt annoyed, thinking of the crowd at the slum and all the journalists who wouldn't leave me alone. After that, we went to the mosque. It wasn't a Friday, but my father wanted us to pray together to thank Allah for what he'd given us. The mosque was empty. Kneeling in the women's section, I enjoyed the quiet atmosphere of the place. I was so grateful to Allah for making me his favourite child. But this calm was short-lived. As soon as we came out of the mosque and headed towards the slum, a bunch of

136

reporters caught up with us again and followed us all the way home. It was a shock when we got there. I was not prepared for such a welcome. It was as if all the residents of Bandra East had gathered near the railway tracks to cheer me. They all ran towards the car and surrounded it. We could hardly get out. The kids were dancing and shouting, 'Rubiiiina! Jai ho! Jai ho!'

My neighbours and friends were there. Everyone was cheering me and looking at me like I was some kind of goddess. I was happy that all of them were so happy for me. Walking down the flight of stairs marking the entrance to the slums, I felt hands touching me. It was chaos. People tried to get close to me but the journalists were worse. They were jumping on me with their huge cameras. I wanted to kill every single one of them. They were squeezing me from all sides. They were falling on me and I couldn't breathe. Somehow my father got people to move aside so that we could reach my uncle's house. It took us half an hour instead of five minutes to get there. There was a holiday atmosphere in the slum. The music of *Slumdog Millionaire* was playing, people were dancing and it looked like a big party was going on. But with all the travelling and the change of planes, I was exhausted. I wanted to escape. I now realized how many people live in India compared to America. The journalists were having a hard time outdoing each other. They were running and pushing each other just for a picture and an interview with me.

When I reached my uncle's house and sat on the bed trying to comprehend all this, I could hear people screaming outside and trying to get in. They were climbing over each other just to look at me. It felt like my uncle's house could collapse at any moment. The door almost fell off and my aunt had to tell them to behave themselves. I tried to speak about the Oscars and America but there were so many reporters talking at the same time that I got lost. After a while I was so angry with them that I couldn't stop crying. I was tired of saying the same things again and again. I didn't understand what the hurry was all about. It seemed to me that they felt that if they didn't speak to me *right now* then the world would collapse.

'How was America? How was America?'

The street outside my uncle's house is very narrow. It's about three foot wide with a sewer running down the middle. We're used to finding our way through this maze of winding lanes, but all the reporters pushing each other to get to me first forgot all about the sewers and drains. All of a sudden, I heard a woman scream. For a brief second, the attention was moved from me. I realized that a reporter had slipped on the damp ground and her foot had landed in the sewer. This was liquid rubbish with bacteria for topping. You had to be very careful where you put your feet. The journalist pulled her foot from this dirty liquid with a horrified expression. She was shouting, 'I have to clean myself up right now! Have you got any water, any soap? Please help me, quickly!'

The woman was not just disgusted, she was frightened. She looked as if she'd faint at any moment. She cleaned herself up as best as she could with a little water my uncle gave her. This was the only thing I found amusing. I thought they deserved it. In fact, I wanted a few others to fall in the ditch. My father was worried for me. He tried to explain that all these journalists were here because I'm an important person now.

'Rubina, why are you so upset?'

'I don't know. I don't understand what these people want from me.'

'They're interested in you. It's only natural.'

'But I don't know what to say to them! I won't be able to do it!'

'Calm down.'

The lane outside my uncle's house and even the next two lanes along were full of reporters. Then Aba finally went out to talk to them.

'Rubina will answer all your questions, but you can only see her one by one.'

Lying on my uncle's bed, I gave interviews until my mouth was dry and I was bored of repeating the same things. I just wanted to go to sleep. I was exhausted, but what could I do? These people refused to go. What they all wanted was some proof that they had spoken to me. I was so fed up.

'Rubina, what did you eat, who did you meet?'

Between interviews, I had to go outside to pose for photos. There was still a huge crowd out there and the queue didn't seem to be getting any shorter. Some were waiting on the road for the crowd to thin out so they could get in. The reporters who couldn't push their way in to speak to me were busy taking pictures of the slum, which fascinated everyone except the people who live here. One journalist almost dropped his camera in the sewer, another, his notebook, and a third, his mic! After the luxury I'd experienced for the past few days, I understood their disgust. Even I was apprehensive about going back to my filthy little streets.

Around 11 p.m., my father asked them to pack up, but still they were saying, 'Please. Please.' I was falling asleep and I didn't care any more.

'My apologies to everyone but Rubina has had a long day and she needs to get some sleep. My daughter will give some more interviews tomorrow.'

Some of them were complaining as they left, others were more understanding. My father took me home, two streets away, and I collapsed on the mat placed on the floor surrounded by my brothers and sisters, without even the strength to exchange a few words with them. The next morning, Munni prepared chai at 7 a.m. My brothers had gone to fetch water from my grandmother, as they did every morning. They were the ones who warned me.

'Rubina, all the reporters are here.'

'Who?'

'People with cameras, lots of them.'

These people were certainly determined. I wasn't likely to be getting any playtime soon. The day was just like the one before: filled with interviews. And the next day was exactly the same. My father and family were also in demand. If the media couldn't speak to me for long, then they moved on to ask my family questions. On the other side of the street, Azhar was also followed by reporters. They wanted to know everything about our lives and our daily existence in the slums. The inhabitants of Bandra were quite flattered by the interest in them.

For three days, journalists filmed the streets and houses in the neighbourhood, questioning many of our neighbours. Finally, when they left, my friends could visit me. My uncle, Mohiuddin, told them in great detail about our trip. Sana and Abbas, and all my friends who hadn't had a chance to ask me any questions, now spent time with me. They wanted to know every single little detail about America: the stars we met on the red carpet, the prize ceremony, Disneyland. Everyone here was very proud of *Slumdog Millionaire*.

The whole slum, who had never even heard of the Oscars before, had been glued to the screen on Oscars night as if it was an India–Pakistan cricket match. The ceremony was broadcast live, which was 4 a.m. in India. Those who had a television set invited the neighbours over to watch. No one wanted to miss the show. Azhar's father had even rented an old set, which he put on the common ground in front of his shack so that everyone could watch it. Again, reporters were there to capture the reactions of the people of the slums. My parents watched the show at my uncle and aunt's house, with the rest of the family and all the neighbours who managed to fit in.

Everyone was excited, even though they didn't understand English at all except 'Slumdog Million-aire' and a few other words. Munni was so tense about the results that she couldn't eat the whole evening. When they finally announced that the Best

Film award goes to *Slumdog Millionaire*, they shouted with joy and hugged each other. My family was very happy to see me on stage with the rest of the crew. They thought I looked lovely. The reactions were quite like the bit in the film when Prem, the presenter of the television gameshow *Kaun Banega Crorepati?*, announces that Jamal Malik has just won 20 million rupees. Seeing a slum kid receiving an international award in a country like America created euphoria in the slum. The news spread like a fire. In a few minutes, even people who couldn't watch the awards on television came to congratulate my father. People were dancing to 'Jai Ho' and giving out sweets to celebrate the event. My father rushed to the mosque the next day to say special prayers to Allah for his blessing on me.

In one evening, I'd become the object of everyone's attention. Everyone seemed to know my first name and where I lived. People called out to me in the street, strangers were greeting me, asking how I was. I was like a princess of the slum. A few days after I got back, to my father's great surprise, Khursheed, my biological mother, showed up.

'What are you doing here?'

'I've come to see Rubina. I haven't seen her in ages.'

'Now you're interested in your daughter? After

143

all these years? There's no way you can see her. Get lost!'

My mother came back the following day, but I refused to see her. That woman was a stranger to me. Now she only cared about me because I was famous. She wanted to have her share of the limelight.

People went crazy over those Oscars. At school, Azhar and I were given a huge welcome. We were portrayed as an inspiration to others. The teacher made us stand in front of the class and talk about our trip. We were flooded with questions from all the other pupils.

The whole slum looked up to us. It was in the grip of Oscar mania.

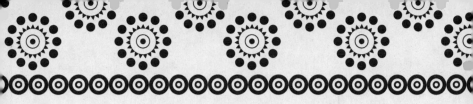

9

My new life

Since the Oscars, my father's new telephone hasn't stopped ringing. There are foreign journalists requesting interviews as well as various other work offers. As soon as we got back to school, Azhar and I had to miss some classes again for another film. This time shooting took only a couple of days. It was a small role in a movie called *Kal Kisne Dekha* (*Who Has Seen Tomorrow*). I don't know what this movie is about. We just had a few scenes in which Azhar and I are coming back from America after the Oscars. At Mumbai airport there is a bomb threat. The hero is trying to move people out. He rushes us out of the airport and saves our lives. It was funny playing ourselves in a movie. But it was a typical Bollywood scene, where the hero saves everyone except the bad

145

guys. The movie had new stars and I didn't know any of them.

We had barely finished the filming when Azhar and I flew to New Delhi to appear in a fashion show for designers Ashima and Leena. Now I was going to be a model, which was perfect because I love dressing in pretty clothes. Azhar's mother accompanied us, along with my father. When we arrived, we were taken to a five-star hotel. We had this huge room with a nice view. I was getting used to such amazing hotels and they didn't surprise me so much any more. It's great going to new places. My father told me Delhi is the capital of India and I was excited about seeing it.

At the hotel, my father had to meet someone from our community so he left me alone. As soon as he'd gone, I slipped on my nightdress and went to sleep with Azhar and his mother. The next morning, I ate my breakfast in a hurry so I could go and visit the swimming pool. I quickly ran back up to the room.

'Azhar!'

'What?'

'Hurry up – there's a swimming pool!'

We didn't stay in the water for long. My father yelled at us, 'Rubina, Azhar, get out of there at once! You have to meet Sonia Gandhi! Now go and get dressed quickly – everyone is waiting for you!'

From the sound of my father's voice, it was no good arguing. I knew that today would be a very busy day as we had to meet Sonia Gandhi, who is a very big *neta* (politician), and then I'd have the fitting of my dress. Then, in the evening, was our fashion show. I'd never been to a fashion show but I'd seen them in this movie called *Fashion* so I knew a bit about what to expect.

There was a car waiting for us downstairs and we left in a hurry. No one keeps a big politician waiting. On the way my father told me that Sonia Gandhi is the President of the Congress party. We passed many important sites and my father pointed out India Gate to me. It has a very beautiful park around it, full of people and a boating area as well. Delhi, I thought, was less crowded than Mumbai. To reach Sonia Gandhi's house, we drove along some beautiful roads full of big trees.

Finally, we reached Sonia Gandhi's house, a huge house with armed guards everywhere. That's normal, when you're as important as Sonia Gandhi. We went through I don't know how many security checks before being allowed to go inside. We were taken in to a large sitting room full of photographs. She was sitting on a sofa, reading a book. When we arrived, all these dogs came and started circling us. I even saw a parrot! A gentleman from security warned us not to get too close to the dogs as they could bite. Those dogs were huge and fat, three times the size of dogs in our slum.

Azhar and I were quite intimidated, as much by these big animals as by the nicely dressed lady coming towards us with a big smile.

'Rubina, Azhar, welcome to my home. I am delighted to meet you.'

'How do you do, ma'am?'

'Thank you for coming all this way. I wanted to congratulate you on the work you have done in this film.'

A handshake, a few smiles and a picture. The meeting didn't last long. She tried to reassure us that everything would be fine and then we left. But I was very proud to meet such an important political figure. I could tell my friends that I'd met her and even been to her house. After the meeting, we went to Ashima and Leena's house for our fittings. It was a huge house, unquestionably the most beautiful one I'd ever seen. In the garden, they had their own swimming pool and two enormous statues of elephants. The house was full of gorgeous ornaments, carpets and furniture. The walls were beautiful colours and everything was perfect. Even the plates and glasses matched. Ashima was a charming lady.

As soon as we arrived, she invited us to sit down

at a table and eat. She had prepared chicken biryani. At Sonia Gandhi's residence we didn't eat anything. I was very hungry and glad to be offered some food. After lunch, Ashima and Leena took us in to the sitting room to show us the clothes we were going to wear in the evening. They were a mixture of Indian and Western styles, very chic and colourful. For Azhar, they had a black *sherwani* embroidered with red designs, over matching trousers. But it was my outfit that I fell in love with: a colourful shimmering gypsy skirt, long and full, made up of seven or eight layers of fabric. It had so many colours: red, green, blue, orange and many more. For a top it had a little sleeveless blouse studded with multicoloured stones. I'd never seen a dress like this before. They told me it was an exclusive piece they'd designed just for me. That made me giggle so much. It was amazing and it fit me well.

'Go ahead, try to move now. This evening, you'll be on a very long catwalk.' They explained this to us. We have to walk down this long stage and when we get to the end, we pose for a few seconds, turn so that everyone sees the clothes from every angle, then walk back in the opposite direction.

I practised. I took a few steps, hands on hips, trying to be graceful and smiley. Following Ashima's directions, I tried to pose and take a turn at the end, and my dress swirled with it. She said, 'Perfect, Rubina.' Azhar, on the other hand, didn't look very much at ease. When I saw him walk, he was stiff and he forgot all his turns. I couldn't help but laugh. I kept spinning to make my skirt twirl around me.

'I love this skirt – it's so beautiful!'

'I'm happy you like it, Rubina. It looks beautiful on you.'

'Can I keep it?'

'Of course – it's yours.'

There can't be many people with a skirt as wonderful as this. I will pose in it for my friends at my house. And then who knows? After all the fancy places I've been to lately, maybe I'll have other functions to attend.

After the fittings, there was a round of interviews with journalists. Azhar sat on the elephant outside to speak to them but I was scared of getting dirty. We were taken back to our hotel to rest. After a while, we went to another grand hotel where the fashion show would take place. It was a big event, full of beautiful people and clothes.

They took us backstage to get ready. It was full of activity. A make-up artist powdered my face, then put some red blush on my cheeks and coloured my lips with a pink gloss. They put a *maang-tikka* in my hair.

It had a huge coral-coloured stone hanging down and it went really well with the whole outfit. Then I put on the skirt and vest and the last accessory: a heavy belt made up of large multicoloured stones. I was ready. I couldn't stop admiring myself in the mirror!

I ran to the other side of the room to watch the fashion models getting ready. They were very pretty, and very tall, in high heels and magnificent outfits. Some wore very long silk or velvet saris in red, blue or green, and also kurtas embroidered with sequins, pearls and stones. They smiled at me, and some even complimented me on my dress. When the show began, the atmosphere became electric and people began rushing around. Azhar and I were a bit anxious. Finally, we were pushed on to the catwalk. The first notes of 'Jai Ho', which was our background music, got us going and then there was no stopping us. I enjoyed the feeling so much.

We had taken only a few steps when the audience began to clap and shout. At the end of the catwalk, I spun a couple of times and gave a few poses to the camera. The reporters kept saying, 'One more, Rubina.' Azhar stood like a tree, looking up with his hands on his hips, as if he were Amitabh Bachchan in person. There was a great atmosphere, everyone was hooting, and then we danced a bit to 'Jai Ho', to the great delight of the audience, who stood up and cheered. In the hall, people were singing 'Jai Ho' at the tops of their voices! We kept posing or dancing and stayed much longer than we were supposed to. Ashima and Leena had to come looking for us and joined us in the mad euphoria.

After the show, journalists came up to ask our reactions, wanting to know what we had thought of it all and the outfits we were wearing. After that, many people came to compliment us or ask us for our autographs. My father enjoyed the show and couldn't stop telling me how great I was. We just had time to eat a bit at the dinner afterwards. It was a fantastic show and our designers were very happy and thanked us again. We said our goodbyes with a promise to meet again. We were taken back to the hotel, where we packed and left for the airport. We took an evening flight back to Mumbai. It had been an amazing day. I was sure my family would have watched the show back home, but I was eager to show them my dress.

I didn't spend much time in Bandra slum as I was leaving again, for Udaipur in Rajasthan this time, to film a commercial for a drink with Nicole Kidman. I was excited about discovering new places. As for Nicole Kidman, I remembered this really tall and milky fair lady I had run into on the red carpet in Los Angeles. Natasha *didi* from the production team of *Slumdog Millionaire* had called my father with this offer. I jumped with joy. Not only was I going to be in an advertisement with a Hollywood star, but also with Arjun Rampal. He is a big star now and I particularly liked him in the movie *Om Shanti Om*, which also has Shahrukh Khan. In this movie, Arjun Rampal plays the role of the bad guy. This time, Azhar was not going to be there – that made me very happy. For this five-day trip, it was my Uncle Mohiuddin who was coming with me. It also gave me confidence that I would have a familiar face on the shoot, Natasha *didi*.

Udaipur airport was much smaller than the others I'd been to. There was a man dressed in a costume who greeted us when we came off the plane. We were taken directly to the film location, at the Taj Lake Palace Hotel, the former palace of a real maharajah converted into a luxury hotel. It was right in the middle of the lake. To get there, a boat came to pick us up. It was a nice boat with a cloth cover on top as a shade. I had already taken a boat in Kolkata to my stepmother Munni's village. This time, it was a private boat! When I looked around, I realized that this place was full of palaces, all of them really big and really beautiful. People must get lost in these huge palaces all the time. How much fun would it be to play hide-and-seek in a place like this. It was like a fairytale land. I told myself that if I had to choose the most beautiful spot in the world to live, it would be here.

At the hotel, I was taken in to a room where I met the crew. I immediately saw Natasha, the make-up artist from *Slumdog Millionaire*. I was so happy to see her again! I hugged her immediately. Nicole Kidman was seated on a sofa, her long golden hair falling down her back, looking a bit lost. When I came in, she stood up and came over to me, incredibly beautiful in her long, white dress.

'Hello, I am so pleased to meet you. How are you?'

'Well, thank you.'

After a few months of learning at the Aseema School, I could now say a few basic sentences in English. But it's always very hard for me to understand when people speak English back to me as they speak very differently from my teachers. Nicole Kidman looked like a beautiful doll. I had never met any woman this tall. All the women from my slum would be so small in front of her. But her skin, lips and hands, they were all perfect. I thought if I touched her, she might get dirty. Arjun Rampal was there, too. When I shook his hand, he praised me so much for my acting in *Slumdog Millionaire* that I blushed! Finally, the director of the advertisement came over to introduce himself.

'Hello, I'm Shekhar.'

'Hello, I'm Rubina.'

'Oh, I know. I've heard a lot about you, you know!'

As for me, I'd never heard of this Shekhar Kapur, but Natasha *didi* told me he's one of the greatest directors. In a few words, Shekhar explained to me what this advertisement was about.

'This is an advertisement to promote a new ginger-flavoured soft drink. The film only lasts two minutes, and your role is important. Natasha is going to make you up and then I'll tell you what you have to do.'

I wondered who drinks ginger-flavoured cold drinks, but they have all kinds of strange food and drink in America so it was no real surprise to me. After the make-up, a lady came to help me put on a long black skirt with a little red blouse embroidered with pearls, a typical Rajasthani dress, they told me. The hairdresser plaited my hair around my temples and placed a heavy silver *maang-tikka* on my head. I also wore a silver belt round my waist and a heavy necklace. The whole look was truly magnificent, much more than Nicole Kidman's, I thought. She just wore a white dress with very little make-up.

Hearing me going crazy over the outfit, the dresser

said: 'You know, after the filming, you can take this dress home with you, if you want.'

'Oh, thank you!'

Another fairytale dress for myself. Wow. Shekhar uncle briefed me on my role. I was to walk amid dancers just admiring and looking at Nicole Kidman. Then I was supposed to hold her hand and run, not too fast, along a passage in the hotel. We then had to climb downstairs, still holding hands. We stand on a platform and there is water in front of us as well as a boat. After that, Nicole lets go of my hand and I touch her, marvelling at the jewels and her beauty. I have to behave completely awestruck by her looks. Then I place a light touch on her cheek as if to make sure she's real, then I smile and watch her leave on the boat. After that, I appear again when she is having this ginger drink.

That was it for the day. The camera test was to be held the next morning. They told me that for security reasons Nicole Kidman wanted to film only between 6 p.m. and 6 a.m. I didn't understand why, so Natasha *didi* told me that it's because she is such a famous star and she's concerned that paparazzi will follow her. Also, she doesn't want to be recognized by the public and wants to maintain her privacy. In the evening, there aren't so many people around and it's also less hot. I found the reasons rather amusing.

First of all, paparazzi sounded like some kind of pizza people would eat in America. But Natasha *didi* told me paparazzi are photographers who take pictures of celebrities when they are unaware.

I found Nicole Kidman strange but also very charming. Everything was done on the set according to her desires and mood. Today was just a briefing and location inspection. It was quite late when I went back to my hotel. Unlike Nicole Kidman, I was not staying in that big lake hotel but in town. It was night when we arrived. It was a very nice hotel, with a palace look and beautiful rooms with lots of candles. Two rooms were booked for us, one for my uncle and the other for me. Each room had a television, a refrigerator filled with drinks and chocolate, and a huge bed. My uncle went to bed, and I stayed alone in my room. It was at that moment that I missed Azhar. If he and his mother had been there, I could have gone and slept with them. I was scared about sleeping alone so I decided to leave the light on. I got in to bed thinking of tomorrow and nervously waited to fall asleep . . .

The next morning, I jumped out of bed, glad still to be alive. I went down to have breakfast with my uncle.

'You know, Rubina, we're in no hurry. The filming doesn't begin until late, and they won't come looking for you before the end of the morning. So you can have fun!'

I didn't even go back up to the room, but rushed straight to the terrace and the swimming pool. There was a beautiful view from there. The sunny weather was perfect for bathing and I didn't want to waste time. But there was no Jacuzzi or small swimming pool like the one in America. I'm not a good swimmer and the water looked very deep. My swimming plans were crushed. I rushed back to my room to eat some cookies and watch television. Finally, in the afternoon I went to the Lake Palace. I was bored there as shooting didn't start until the evening. I roamed around the hotel, up and down between floors and round the lovely gardens. I saw some multicoloured glass windows, which were really beautiful. I enjoyed looking through them and seeing how they made things appear in different colours. I ate, but the food wasn't that great so I filled myself up with different coloured cold drinks. Fortunately, Natasha came looking for me to get ready. Nicole Kidman had finally arrived. She didn't come out even once during the afternoon. She just came down for her shot and then ran back to her room.

Natasha said, 'She's not too well. It's probably too hot for her. She prefers to stay in her room.'

I would have liked to play and chat with her a bit. That evening we rehearsed our sequence of shots. They asked me to think about the expressions on my face. I also did a bit of dancing in the opening shot. But mostly there were professional Rajasthani dancers dressed in local costume, much more professional than Nicole and me. I loved watching them, the way they turned and twirled. In films, the dance scenes have always been my favourites. I watched the dancers quite closely as I wanted to pick up some steps to teach my cousins back home. Shekhar uncle and I became friends and he was quite happy with my work. The only thing I didn't like were the long waits because of the American star.

Like the night before, I got back to my hotel quite late. The next day, I hung around in my hotel with nothing much to do till evening. This time, we filmed in our costume. Nicole Kidman wore the same white dress I'd seen her in the first day. A magical sort of thin white cloth covered her shoulders. She wore beautiful jewels and Natasha *didi* told me they were real diamonds. Between each shot, the star took big breaks with all her assistants around her. She had so many assistants, along with plenty of bodyguards. When she was present, she spoke very little. I got bored quite quickly. The following days went by in the same way. Afraid of the heat, Nicole Kidman stayed in her room all day, whereas I just walked round and round. By the end I knew every corner of the hotel and had made friends with some of the staff too. But the food didn't agree with me. It was quite similar to American food. I think my grandmother and aunt are the best cooks in the world. I had to make do with Coca-Colas and ice creams.

Those five days were so long! I couldn't wait to get this shoot over and head back to my friends.

10

For sale

One day out of the blue my father told me that someone had come from very far away just to meet me. I
asked my father who it was.

'The wife of an Arabian sheikh!'

'What's a sheikh, Aba?'

'It's a sort of prince – very rich. They live in Dubai.
His wife wants to meet you.'

'Dubai? Where's that?'

'It is quite far from Mumbai but not as far as
America.'

My aba told me that she was totally in love with
me after watching my performance in *Slumdog
Millionaire*. She'd even cried watching the movie.
Apparently, she had called before my America trip
and invited me and my family to Dubai to spend a

161

few days with them, but Aba had refused the invitation as we didn't even have passports then and she was a complete stranger to us.

But now I was delighted to have a fan who had come all the way from a different country to meet me. The big politicians had congratulated me, famous Bollywood actors appreciated my work and journalists from all over the world came to interview me, but no one had ever come this far before just because they loved me in the movie. And this was no ordinary fan but an Arab princess as well. I found it a bit hard to believe, but then I was not an average star. On the contrary, I was a very famous one. My father smiled at my confusion.

'So you want to meet her?'

'Of course . . . Is she going to come to the house?'

'Even better: she's inviting us to her hotel – a five-star hotel.'

I loved luxury hotels and knew what to expect. They are full of unusual corners and there's always some means of having fun. I ran straight to my cousins' house to tell them. My cousins have heard many stories about five-star hotels and this time Mohsin wanted to see for himself. He was really excited about the idea of coming with us to meet the sheikh's wife.

'Hey, Rubina, do you think I can come with you?'

'I don't know. Ask your father.'

My father and uncle readily agreed to let him come with us. He took ages deciding what to wear. He was glued to the mirror, combing his hair in different styles. We went there in the evening. There were quite a few of us, including my uncle, cousin, Aba and a distant relative called Uncle Rajan. We went in two rickshaws and it took almost an hour to reach the Leela Hotel. It's a really big palace, more luxurious than the one in Juhu. I was wearing a pretty orange and white dress.

In the hotel lobby, a man with a black beard came to greet us. He introduced himself as the personal secretary to the sheikh, who, unfortunately, was not able to come. He was very friendly and invited us to have something to eat. My father, like me, doesn't like the food of five-star hotels so we just ordered some tea. After that, we followed the man with the beard to the sheikh's wife's room, where we were greeted by a woman veiled entirely in a black burqa. I was eager to meet my crazy fan. She was from the same religion as us.

'Welcome, Rubina, I'm so pleased to meet you!'

'Hello!'

She seemed nice. She invited us to sit on the sofas. While everyone else sat down, I did a quick tour of this huge, luxurious room.

Rajan uncle translated for us. He can speak English.

'Children, would you like to have something? You can order whatever you want.'

'Can we have an ice cream?'

'And a strawberry milkshake?'

'Anything you wish. I'll order right now.'

The sheikh's wife looked at me as if I was the seventh wonder of the world. She never stopped complimenting me on my role in *Slumdog Millionaire*.

'Oh, Rubina, if you knew how I cried when I saw the film! You were fantastic!'

I started to blush. The lady was asking me so many questions, wanting to know everything about the filming. Aba has always been very proud of me and he told her about the auditions that Danny uncle organized in Mumbai to find the young actors for his film, and how I was chosen from over five hundred children. She shook her head in admiration while we were busy exploring the room. Finally, our milkshakes and ice cream arrived. Mohsin and I were having fun, especially Mohsin, who'd never been to a place like this before. We finished our drinks and felt very content while the adults continued talking between themselves through the help of Rajan uncle.

'Hey, did you see the plasma screen on the wall?'

'And the bed – did you ever see such a big bed?'

In my American hotel, the bed was as big as this, even slightly bigger. We went over and sat on the edge of the soft mattress and tried a little jump to test its softness. The Arab princess was amused. She called me over and gave me three large boxes of chocolates. Mohsin also came over to see what it was. I opened one straight away and passed them around, not forgetting to eat some myself along the way. I love chocolates! The lady also gave me a gold-coloured chain with a pendant. She made me sit in front of her and fastened it round my neck. I didn't know if it was gold but, in any case, it was pretty. For a few minutes, I admired my new piece of jewellery, looking at myself in the mirror. However, my father intervened.

'Rubina, take that off now.'

'But why?'

'Rubina, please! We cannot accept a gift like that.'

At least I still had my chocolates. My father and uncles decided to leave as it was getting quite late. Before leaving I asked her casually whether we could come back the next day.

'But of course, Rubina, come back and bring your family for lunch if you like.'

'Thank you . . . See you tomorrow then!'

Chances to get out of the slum are rare. Late the next morning, we were back at the Leela Hotel. This time, Rajan's daughter, Reshma, was also with us, along with Munni, who'd put on her best *salwar kameez*, and a young neighbour. After Mohsin's description, no one wanted to miss the opportunity to visit such an amazing place. I wore the jeans I'd brought back from America. Like the day before, the sheikh's secretary was waiting for us in the lobby. He escorted us to the princess's room. She was waiting for me and took me in to the bedroom next door, and we left the men to talk among themselves. Once we were alone, I picked up the remote control, asking the princess with my eyes if I could use it.

'Go ahead, enjoy yourself!'

I spent fifteen minutes going through all the television channels: there were so many! Then me and my cousin Reshma explored the place a bit. Reshma was quite taken aback with the grandness of it all. I loved seeing the expressions on her face.

Finally, the sheikh's secretary called us. 'Are you hungry, children?'

'Yeeesss!'

'The restaurant is this way. A vast spread of food awaits you.'

I ran fast and tried to slide on the slippery floor. They'd reserved a large table for us at the back of the restaurant. In the middle of the room was a truly enormous buffet. I was starving and wanted to taste everything. Before long I had a mountain of food on my plate! Even when we were all full there were still sweets to be explored. I couldn't help but stuff myself with pastries, drinking glass after glass of mango juice. I don't think I've ever eaten so much in my life. After that we went back to the princess's room, where my father, the princess and Rajan were in conversation. My father sounded angry but I couldn't understand what was going on. At last, my father announced it was time to leave. I realized he wasn't looking very comfortable any more. As we were leaving the hotel, he barely opened his mouth. On the way back to the slums, I questioned him.

'Aba, what's wrong?'

'Nothing. Those people are not right.'

'Why?'

'In the room, the secretary told me this princess couldn't have children and wanted to adopt you.'

'Adopt me? What for?'

'He told me that if you grew up in Dubai, you'd receive a good education and have a fine life. He even offered me a great deal of money.'

'But I don't want to go to Dubai!'

'I know, and that's what I told them – that I am not going to part with my daughter.'

Suddenly, I understood why my father looked so angry. As soon as we got home, I rushed off to see my cousins and tell them about our adventure. For me, this was just another thing to tell my friends about. But I wasn't happy about what those people had tried to do. I'd heard stories from neighbours and my uncle about rich people trying to buy children, then making them slaves or using them for prostitution. I have seen bad things happening to people, like really young girls being married to really old men. Whenever I go out and see a kid begging it saddens me. I know it's hard for them to manage even a meal a day. On the other side of the slum, some people live in a gutter. You have to crawl to get inside and it's pitch dark and smells. It's terrible, with no air and with drain water dripping, but they have nowhere else to go. I feel privileged to have such good parents. I know they'll do anything for me. But that night I had a bad dream about being separated from my family and taken to a place I'd never been to. I woke up scared and was glad it was just a bad dream.

Then the next Sunday morning, police turned up at our house. I didn't even for a moment imagine it could have anything to do with the sheikh's wife. I didn't understand what was going on. There were journalists making a queue as well and my father's phone didn't stop ringing. Munni was worried. Then my father realized that those people in the hotel had told everyone about our meeting and said that my father had tried to sell me. The police wanted my father to go to the station with them. He was shocked, and went with them, with me close on their heels as far as the slum entrance. The whole slum turned up to see what was going on. Because it was a Sunday morning people had nothing much to do, so this provided them with entertainment.

Apparently, my biological mother had filed a case against my father, accusing him of trying to sell me. After my father's statement they let him go. Aba looked very tense. We all felt cheated by that fake sheikh and his partner. My family and I have always trusted people. I was angry and ready to fight with everyone.

'Rubina, that lady at the Leela Hotel was a false princess. Those people were just pretending to come from Dubai but really they were journalists trying to get us into trouble. They wrote an article on a foreign website with a computer, accusing me of wanting to sell you. Someone informed Khursheed, and she lodged a complaint against me, demanding your custody. That's why the police wanted to question me.'

That lying fake princess. I could hardly believe

that someone would do something like that. But my biological mother's antics were making me even more angry. She really is mad! She turned up at the slum and created a big scene, abusing my father and the whole family.

'I want to see my daughter! I want to speak to Rubina immediately!'

I hid in our room.

'Rubina! I know you're in there! Come out.'

'No. I don't want to see you!'

'Rubina, don't believe what you hear about me. Your father lies to you!'

My father wasn't there, but Munni, my stepmother, came out. My biological mother yelled even louder: 'You bitch! I know you tried to sell my daughter! I won't let you get away with it. I want custody of Rubina!'

When Munni replied to her accusations, Khursheed jumped on her. My stepmother was three months pregnant at that time and Khursheed tried to harm her physically. They began fighting in the narrow lane, in front of the neighbours and a TV camera. Khursheed and Munni were kicking each other. Khursheed shoved my stepmother violently. It was the neighbours who separated them. My biological mother was accusing Munni of having done black magic on me. Munni comes from West Bengal, which is famous for its black magic. I've heard about people doing black magic in slums because they're jealous of each other. There are women who specialize in such things. They take a piece of worn cloth or a strand of hair from the person they want to do black magic on. This is common in Mumbai but in Bengal the people doing such things live in burning *ghats* and it's all much more serious. But I knew my Munni Ami wasn't like this and that she loved me and my father.

I lay low. I felt really upset over what was going on outside. Now, the truth seems to have come out and my father's name has been cleared. As for my biological mother, I hate her more than ever. I am not for sale, and whoever claims I am is a liar. Just because we are poor does not mean my father would do anything for money. He is not like that. He is an honourable man. But many in the slum are not, and every day there are fights about money. But my aba loves me. He would never part with me for anything in the world.

ii

I hate cockroaches

Life hasn't changed much for me except that now I'm aware of a world much more beautiful than my slum. After the comforts of hotels and star treatments, I was back to playing in the dirt and dreaming. The advertisement with Nicole Kidman and the fashion show in Delhi each earned me something like 80,000 rupees. My father knew nothing about this industry and that's why he didn't negotiate well. For *Slumdog Millionaire*, he signed the contract on whatever was offered. In the end, I got something like 40,000 in hand. It was even less than this at first, but since filming took longer than expected, the production company handed out more money on a daily basis. I got the money in instalments of 4,000 or 5,000 rupees.

173

Azhar earned more money than me because his father fought with Parvesh and didn't just accept whatever was offered. With Azhar's mother on the set, Parvesh couldn't cheat them. In the end they managed to get around 150,000, four times more than I did. Almost all the money I got from *Slumdog* went on the medical expenses for my father's broken ankle. I'm sure I was given more than 40,000 but I'm not sure if I got all of it, or where it has all gone. So, I still lived in a little shanty, ate simple food and played on the railway track. It was all the same except for our only indulgence: a new flatscreen television. As my house was too small, we put the flatscreen in my uncle Mohiuddin's house. Now, I spend most of my time at my uncle's house. I think our family is the only one in the slum with this kind of television.

Aba opened an account in my name in a bank in Bandra. He wanted me to save money for my future. I don't know much about money and banks. The only difference now is that it's easy to get a few extra rupees out of him! Before, I used to buy inexpensive clothes and shop only two or three times a year, but now I go shopping every week with Ami and Aba and can buy dresses as expensive as 800 rupees. I always come back with something: a bag, a toy, a skirt. Before, Aba would never let me treat myself like this, but now I think I'm a little independent in my spending. At home, I keep my clothes in plastic bags that Ami hangs from hooks on the wall. There's a bag for new clothes, a bag for old clothes and a bag for designer clothes. I change clothes several times a day.

'What's the point of all these clothes? Look, you can't even make up your mind!'

I don't care; I love to look nice. All the actresses wear nice clothes all the time. I loved the shopping experience in America, though the clothes there don't have as much embroidery or as many shiny sequins. They are much paler and quieter-looking. I brought my father a T-shirt back from America on which it says, 'A T-shirt can save the world'. A journalist told me what it meant since I didn't understand it. Now I know that clothes can't save the world, but they've changed my life. If you're well dressed, people look at you differently. I love being complimented on how I look. I even put on a special cream called Fair and Lovely so as not to get dark in the sun. Ami insists on using it too. I don't want to get dark. All the Bollywood actresses are so fair. In the slum, too, everyone prefers a fair girl to a dark one. They say you get a better husband if you are fair.

Right now, I'm young, and that's why I can wear anything. But in the slums after a certain age girls don't wear Western clothes. People would make fun of them and boys would think they're cheap. Around the age of fifteen most girls start to cover up with a burqa. I think even I will have to wear a burqa. My father really wants me to. My grandmother tells me a good woman or a girl always covers herself. My cousin Rukhsar already wears one whenever she leaves the house to go to school or meet her friends. Not all Muslim women wear the burqa. My aunt, for example, dresses normally. Sometimes she even wears jeans because my uncle has no problem with it. My father wants me to start wearing a burqa when I'm twelve or thirteen. I like the burqa, but then I've never seen actresses with their heads covered. I'm confused, really. Sometimes I want to wear a burqa because Aba wants me to, but then I love to flaunt my clothes as well. Another thing I know is that my family wouldn't like if I wore very small clothes like the heroines on screen these days. I shall have to choose my movie roles carefully.

I love wearing make-up. I think all the girls I know do. I have my own make-up now, lipsticks, powder and nail polish. Before I used to look through my ami's things and try them on. My favourites are kohl and eyeliner. I also like jewellery, but I don't have many things, only some colourful plastic bangles. But my father has promised to buy me a real gold chain and a silver ring. I like having henna motifs on my hands and Rukhsar is really good at doing it; even my neighbours come to her on special occasions. My dream is to wear blue contact lenses one day and have eyes like the snake goddess. A few weeks ago my cousins Mohsin and Rukhsar went to a photography studio to get their pictures taken. Mohsin wanted the pictures to send to different directors. But for Rukhsar, they are to send to a boy's family to arrange a match. She wore a very heavy *salwar kameez* and saris with lots of artificial jewels. And those amazing blue contact lenses.

Not long ago, Rukhsar took me to her school's farewell party. All her friends wanted to meet me. I was a star guest! I wanted to look different so I wore my pretty gypsy skirt from the fashion show in New Delhi. I wasn't going to miss a chance like this to show off. I danced my movie songs just like everyone wants me to do wherever I go. My swimming-pool-blue dress from the Oscars is muddy after I tried it on to show everyone in the slums, including visiting journalists. Only my clothes and people's attitudes towards me have changed. Otherwise my life is the same as before.

I don't know anyone living in this slum who wouldn't want to live in a real apartment. The problem is that houses in Mumbai are really expensive. My father recently told me that he read in a newspaper that some houses in Mumbai are more expensive than the ones in New York and London.

My friends have started to tease me.

'So, Rubina, you're a star! What are you doing still in the slums?'

I don't want to leave Mumbai to move somewhere else. If I want to become an actress, Mumbai is the place to be. After the Oscars, loads of people called to congratulate me, including some important people like local councillors. They made us promises and thanked us for being a source of national pride. A local Mumbai co-operative said they would give us two apartments in permanent buildings. A real house with cement walls, windows, somewhere to put my things and a proper toilet is all I want. If someone gave us the keys to an apartment, even a long way from Bandra, I'd move immediately. I want a better life where I can think of improving myself and achieving much more. In a slum, life is about survival. I'd really miss my friends, my grandmother and my cousins, but I could still come and visit them every day.

Since I got back from America, I've been finding this place harder and harder to live in. It's not that safe any more. A few weeks ago, Rukhsar, my cousin, had her mobile stolen while she was sleeping in the afternoon. The thief walked in and picked her phone up, which was charging near the television. It was her birthday present, a very expensive phone with a camera. Since the slums have been full of reporters, people think we've become well off. My aunt, who has a few pieces of gold jewellery, prefers to wear them all the time instead of keeping them in the cupboard. We never had problems with theft in the slums before. Everyone knew each other and trusted each other. My fame seems to have made people jealous. They think a star like me must have some valuable things hidden away. But I don't want my few belongings to be taken away from me.

After America with its beautiful houses, its spotless streets without a single piece of rubbish on the ground and its ultra-clean hotel rooms, I realize how shabby it is here. I don't want something as fancy as America, just something better than my slum, with basic amenities such as a tap with running water and a bed to sleep in. I notice the bad side of life here much more now: the arguing, the people insulting each other all the time and the boys harassing and chasing the girls. I have seen husbands beating their wives and yelling at them. I feel so bad for them.

There are so many cockroaches in the slum. Some can even fly. Sometimes, they fall in our food, but we don't throw the food away, we just throw the cockroach out of it. Two proper meals in a slum is a luxury very few can afford and that's why no one wastes food here. We treat the house regularly with an insecticide that stinks for two or three days afterwards. But the worst things in the slums are rats. They terrify me. There are so many drains and sewers and so much dirt that thousands of rats can survive easily here. They multiply so fast. The most dangerous ones are the big fat ones. They aren't scared of human beings. You can find them on your bed, on your shelves and in the kitchen. I feel dirty just looking at them, but I see many every day. Not long ago, a rat climbed up my calf when I was sitting on the doorstep in front of my house. I was screaming and shaking. Munni pushed it away with a rag, but I shudder just thinking about it.

Mosquitoes are another problem no one in the slum knows how to deal with. At night people either sleep under mosquito nets or cover up with sheets despite the heat so as not to get bitten. Every year, children die of malaria in our slum. My father had it several years ago. He was in bed with a fever for many days and shivered all the time. There are many diseases in the slums. If you go to a proper doctor, not a quack, you'll recover quickly. If it's not malaria, then it's typhoid. My uncle had both in the space of six months: typhoid last year and malaria just before we went to America. So far I've been lucky: I've never caught either. When I was five or six, I was very ill. I think I drank some infected water and my stomach got swollen. I don't know the exact name of this disease but it was deadly. I had to have an operation. I was in hospital for two weeks. Apart from that operation, I've never had anything seriously wrong with me, though I catch a cold during the months of monsoon every year.

The whole of Mumbai comes to a standstill during the monsoons. Some days, it rains continuously and even the railway tracks fill with water. The slums are the worst affected because there's no proper drainage system. In some other area, where the slums were on a hill, during a bad monsoon a few years ago the whole slum collapsed, killing many people. Our slum fills with water up to knee-height during the rains. There are flies everywhere and people get sick. The sheets are always damp and every corner of the house smells. There are long power cuts and walking outside is difficult because you can fall in to unseen holes and break a bone. Some people collect rainwater because the taps are submerged or else broken. You have to store food before the rains come too as everything gets very expensive. Hardly any shops are open. Every year, I hope that I can escape the slums during the monsoon.

The toilet area becomes unbearable during the

rainy season. But rains or no rains, it's always in a bad state. This is a small concrete building with three toilets and no doors. The toilets are holes in the ground with a step on either side for your feet. You have to carry your own mug of water with you to wash. The municipal services are supposed to come and remove the waste from time to time, but no one ever does. The place stinks. Also, you can't see a thing because there's no electricity. Like all the kids, I preferred to go outside near the railway tracks. But I'm too big now to show my backside to the world, though sometimes at night I still go to the tracks for a quick leak. Since I got back from America, I've been going to the pay toilets, ten minutes' walk away. It costs two rupees and it's perfectly clean. If we had our own apartment, I wouldn't need to go any distance to relieve myself.

Last week, Azhar's house was demolished by the local authorities. Apparently he was also beaten up and his fighter *murga* (cock) got killed. I know they didn't give them any notice, they just came and crushed their little shack. I felt very bad for him and was glad it hadn't happened to me and my family. But this happiness and a roof over my head didn't last long. One fine morning the people from the railway authorities came and destroyed my world too. I woke up to the sounds of shouting, and when

I went out my neighbours were having an argument with the authorities. They didn't listen to anyone and destroyed around forty shanties, including ours. No one had been given any notice. My uncle and aunt were out shopping when all this happened. My father got into a fight with the police, who were supervising the demolition, and he got injured. I'm so angry with everyone. They don't even stop to think before smashing up our houses. We've moved to my uncle's house for now, but I don't know where we'll end up.

They can destroy my little slum but I still have my dreams to take me to better and bigger places.

12

'Jai Ho!'

For the following few weeks the news channel
and newspapers were full of the story of how my
father tried to sell me. I started to distrust and
dislike journalists. I heard then that Danny uncle
had told the press that he would provide for Azhar
and me until we come of age. But I couldn't feel
happy because I was shaken by all this commotion,
and so many promises made to me remained
unfulfilled.

The media people, TV cameras and journalists,
were swarming everywhere. They even came to my
little school, which I try to attend daily now. With all
the filming, the fashion show, then the commercial
with Nicole Kidman, I ended up missing a lot of

school. As a result, I have to do my exams separately (with Azhar, who has also missed a lot of school), in April before the start of our holidays. I have been getting many work offers in India and for some the shooting will take place in foreign countries like Switzerland. But nothing is sure and confirmed. My father doesn't mind me working during the holidays but I know he doesn't like it if I miss classes. But if it is a big offer, I'm sure he will come around. But the last six months have taught me and my father a lot about this industry. I don't think we will trust people blindly any more.

I want to become a great actress. If not an actress, I would like to be an astronaut. I know the second option is harder but I know everything is possible with hard work. Later on, I'd like to go to college in America, if my father allows. I think I'm more ambitious now than before. I would like to take private English lessons to improve my language as well. Speaking good English is essential for an actress, and even for an astronaut. This March, I got an offer of writing down my little life story for others to know me better. A French publisher came here to the slums and spent days with us. I like this idea because now I can tell everyone who I really am. But my father was a bit confused about what this book would be, what I would say and who would want to buy it, and so it took him some time to decide. Finally, we signed a contract – and he was happy that everything was done in the proper way. It hasn't been too difficult to talk about myself, my slum, my family, my journey. Many journalists have written false things about me and my family. I know very little about the outside world. Nor does the outside world know anything about my daily life, so this book can let the world know the real Rubina Ali.

Half of the money from this book will go to a big charity near my slum. Some of the book's earnings will buy me dance lessons, singing lessons and even an acting teacher to teach me everything an actress should know. I shall save some for my future education as I know my father has limited means, but finally a proper reward for my work could buy me a better life. And I will also be going to Europe, to France, for the book launch and promotion. I hope my father can come with me. I can't wait to see another new city and to see the friends I have made while working on my book. But I really hope Paris has better food than America. I will try to eat it, even if it doesn't have spices in it. So, Paris, here I come.

Now my dreams are even bigger. And I don't think anyone can stop me reaching the stars if I really try. This is me, Rubina Ali.

Jai Ho!
Mumbai, May 2009

RUBINA ALI is an actress who played the youngest version of Latika in the multi-Oscar-winning *Slumdog Millionaire* (2008), for which she won a Screen Actors Guild Award. Following the film's success, she was cast in the Bollywood film *Kal Kisne Dekha*.

Anne Berthod is a journalist in France.

Divya Dugar is a journalist in India.